NATIONALISM
IN THE SOVIET UNION

NATIONALISM
IN THE
SOVIET UNION

HANS KOHN

AMS Press, Inc.

New York

1966

AMS Press, Inc.
New York, N.Y. 10003
1966

Manufactured in the United States of America

DK
267
K6

DK
267
K613
1966

Ha14070 omq14082

CONTENTS

PREFACE

THE following inquiry is based both on theoretical study and on actual experience of the new atmosphere in Russia during a journey which I made in the summer of 1931 for the *Frankfurter Zeitung*. Contact with the new type of man who is growing up in the Soviet Union, and with his ideas and ideals, has made plain to me to how great an extent the phenomenon of nationalism in the Soviet Union is intellectually part and parcel of the new system of faith and philosophy, and how the problems of nationalism and the efforts to grapple with them can only be understood if considered in relation to the system as a whole. Much less attention, however, has been paid to the problem of nationalism in the U.S.S.R. and the effort to grapple with it than to economic questions, although in Europe and the East alike nationalism continues to this day to be the formative element that it has been in modern historic development, the myth of our epoch, showing itself stronger in times of strong emotional appeal than class and party loyalties, considerations of economic interest, and the personal concern for safety of life and happiness. The way the U.S.S.R. has made its reckoning with nationalism may throw a new light on the nature of nationalism, the course which it is following in our time, and the possibilities of its future development.

This book does not set out to tell a traveller's tale; large numbers of excellent descriptive works have already made the externals of life in the Soviet Union sufficiently familiar. What this book aims at is the presentation of the mentality of the Soviet citizen, of the Communist "theology" and the way in which it has tried to make its peace with the "theology" of nationalism that dominates the world of to-day.

In my book, *Sinn und Schicksal der Revolution* ("The meaning and the fate of the Revolution," published by E. P. Tal, Vienna, 1923), I applied my studies and experiences in Siberia in the years 1916–1919 to the attempt to describe the mental outlook of the men and women of Russia, and to interpret the nature of the Russian Revolution which had been fostered by that outlook and by Western influences. (The first origins of the

Revolution date back to the rising of the Deka-brists a hundred years ago under the influence of the ideas of the French Revolution, brought to Moscow by the Napoleonic wars.) When I wrote that book, however, the principal element in the Revolution was for me the Russian spirit; to-day I see it in Communism and Leninism. Actual contact with the Russian Revolution, as with the French a century and a half ago, is a disturbing and painful experience; it faces the observer time after time with the necessity of revising judgments, destroys old certainties and throws a new and alarming light on tried and trusted relationships. The enormous Eurasian territory that stretches from Poland to the Pacific, and from the Arctic to the gates of India, is turning back past the age of Rationalism and even the Renaissance, past which we cannot retrace our steps and by which its masses have scarcely been touched, to the beliefs of mediæval mankind. More is at issue than the struggle between two economic systems: Communism and Western civilization stand face to face as divergent conceptions of the meaning of life and of human values.

Yet both are rooted in the same basic idea: in

the secularization of the Biblical faith in world history as a single comprehensive conception, a connected whole, and in the recognition of man's own activities as a determining element in the historic process, a recognition which dates from the French Revolution. The Westerner of the last hundred years, to quote a phrase of Karl Jasper's, has "brought men to the mutual recognition of one another and to the consciousness of their fellow-membership in human society." It is only within this last century that man has achieved the conquest and mechanization of Nature, and with an amazing acceleration of pace the Westerner has drawn the whole diminished globe into this process, has paved the way to a planetarization of the new and continually more intricately woven network of economic and cultural interdependence, a planetarization that has robbed nationalism in its modern form and the political order of national States of all solid basis in reality. This œcumenical mission of the nineteenth century—amid all the confusion of the present day, we are witnessing such a growth of unity in humanity as has never been known before—has been taken up by Communism and carried into its reckoning with nationalism.

This dawning of an epoch in which mankind will become conscious of its essential unity reveals the differences between Communism and the West as stages on the road to the future world-wide ordering of human society. So long as that "Great Society" remains unattained, Communism challenges the West, in an incomparably deeper and more spiritual way than America, to an examination of the Western system of life, to reflection on the stamp which the West has placed upon the features of its citizens and has made characteristic of its own nature and history —on the dignity and liberty of the individual for which the West has battled and which it has secured. For "the limit of the world-wide ordering of human society lies in the liberty of the individual, who must achieve by his own efforts what no one can do for him, if humanity is to endure."

H. K.

NATIONALISM
IN THE SOVIET UNION

EAST AND WEST

This war introduces the latest and worst crisis
of Capitalism. If we do not succeed in diverting
its course into revolution it is bound to lead to
further grave crises and wars.

LENIN (August 1914).

The Soviet Union is changing with enormous
speed from a backward country, an agrarian
country, into a progressive country of large-scale
industry.

From the resolutions of the sixteenth
congress of the Communist Party of Soviet
Russia, July 1930.

THE great creative forces of the West, Rome and
mediæval philosophy, the Renaissance and the
Reformation, left the empire of the Tsars of
Russia untouched; the empire drew the forces
for its development from the East. Amid all the
variety of their lingual origins, the peoples of that

B   I

wide realm were related to one another through the racial mixture of Slavonic, Finnish, and Tartar-Mongolian blood. For centuries the country was dominated by Eastern hordes; after their yoke had been shaken off, a constant succession of pioneers crossed the country eastwards, penetrating and linking up plain and steppe and desert as far as the Pacific and the Pamirs. The bold march of conquest of the Cossack Yermak into Siberia in 1581 surpasses in scale the westward treks of the North American colonists; but, unlike the penetration of the Middle and Far West, Russo-Asiatic expansion remained a penetration and nothing more, until the Soviet Government began to awaken the boundless territory into active life. The religions of the Tsarist empire, the Orthodox Church, offspring of Byzantium and sunk in the apathy of the East, and Islam, were in natural harmony with an Oriental theocratic despotism. The welding of the empire did not proceed from Kiev, which had felt the impulse of Rome's last ebbing waves, Kiev whose river flowed down to the Black Sea with its Hellenic past, but from Moscow, whose communications led to Kazan and Astrakhan and the lakes of Asiatic steppes that gave no access to the Mediterranean. From the middle ages until late in the nineteenth century the merchant of Moscow much more closely resembled the merchant of Persia in clothing and habits of life, in his domestic arrangements and his outlook on the world, than the traders of Italy or Holland.

Peter the Great applied a ruthless despotism to the effort to turn his country's face to the West; but he was not thinking of the philosophy or the intellectual refinements of the West, which were strange to him, but of its technical superiority, its organization and exploitation of assembled man-power and natural resources. In his time the women of the Russian nobles were still secluded in harems, and he had to effect their release against the furious opposition of the boyars. Peter's work is being carried forward to-day on an incomparably greater scale by Communism, in a campaign of world-wide significance. Once more an eastern country is being westernized, with a new boldness of conception and systematic thoroughness. ("East" and "West" are not intended here as racial or geographical distinctions—Japan, in the present connexion, belongs to the West—but as broad types of particular stages of historical, social, and cultural development.)

The Capitalism of the nineteenth century dragged the countries outside Europe from their seclusion and isolation and brought them, if only as passive members, within the circle of world trade. In this world-wide synthesis, Capitalism performed a creative task, driving civilization forward. A division of labour and a temporary harmonization was produced between the highly developed industrial states of the West, with their accumulated capital, and the colonial and quasi-colonial countries such as Russia, South America, and the East. The quasi-colonial countries supplied products of the soil and raw materials, and in return imported machinery and formed a market for industrial products and capital investment from the West. Such industries as they had were of the light type. The "western" economic system faced an "eastern" system that supplemented and served it, so that, speaking in terms of world trade, the capitalist West might be regarded as one great city and the rest of the world as its country-side.

Since the world war the efforts of these "eastern" countries to win emancipation have been throwing the capitalist world out of balance. In place of their past passive acceptance of the part assigned to them in world trade, they are out now to secure active participation, setting up their own industries, promoting their independent economic development by a protective tariff policy, and applying technical advance to the service of their own purposes.[1] Along this path the Soviet Union is energetically pursuing its pioneering course.[2] The Five-year Plan aims at converting the Soviet Union from a country economically, technically, and culturally behind the age into a country well abreast of the age and with highly developed industries.

If this economic and technical emancipation is not to be confined, as were the reforms of Peter the Great, to a small upper circle of society, it must be accompanied, in the Soviet Union and in all "eastern" countries, by a psychological and cultural revolution. The achievements of Capitalism and the technical advances of the age of machinery, the introduction of responsible calculation and concern for legality into economic and social relations in emulation of the dominance of law in Nature, were based on a new ethic of labour—originating in the Puritanism of the

Protestant countries of north-west Europe—and
lent a new importance to disciplined labour.   It
was under allegiance to this new spirit that the
Anglo-Saxons and the Dutch entered into the
colonial heritage of the Spanish and the
Portuguese.

The new ethic regarded labour as an ascetic
duty, as the justification of our life on this earth.
The indolent, quasi-instinctive labour of the
naïve "Easterner," with its dilettante enjoyment
of form and colour, was subjected to "sensible"
leadership and responsible discipline.   Work had
until then been the curse of Adam, the lilies of the
field had borne witness to the care-free blessed-
ness of a life "in accordance with nature"; now
indolence was made into the fountain-head of all
vices.   Labour was not vested with nobility, but
it became a duty, and poverty, in the East a
legitimate and often a holy mode of life, became
a reproach and a disgrace.   The duty of labour
produced a new human type, more disciplined
and more controlled than the "natural" man,
than the Russian or the Oriental, more steadfast
and fixed in purpose, cooler and with a better
sense of order and proportion and attention to
detail.   The origins of this new way of living

were religious; it grew, like the ideas of democracy and human rights, in the English Revolution of the seventeenth century, with its Biblical inspiration; its spread was not merely an imperialistic process of conquest, a search for new dominions, but also a missionary enterprise, for the transformation of lives and the salvation of souls. Bourgeois society aimed at a steady incorporation of the whole world in its system, moulded to its own pattern. In this idea of a mission lay the world-wide importance of Anglo-Saxon Imperialism.

Communism is well aware that there is no possibility of industrialization on a grand scale without this ethic of labour. Capitalist Imperialism trained only a small upper section of the colonial and quasi-colonial peoples as technicians and organizers; the great mass of the population were left entirely out of consideration. Here too the Soviet Union is making a radical innovation. It is this purpose that underlies the intensive educative work of the Soviet Government, its concentration on the training and uplifting of the masses, on awakening their initiative and saturating them with a new ethic of labour. Not until this educative work has been done can the "eastern" peoples hope themselves to be able to provide the industrial efficiency and the experience of machinery required for a fully-developed modern economic system. In the East, in South America, in Russia there is a fatalistic acceptance of backwardness to be combated, a pleasure in self-reliance and in the active use of their own brains to be awakened in the masses; the social foundations of life have to be radically reconstructed, women's emancipation to be achieved and their active interest enlisted in public affairs. In this educational work, the Soviet Union is proving itself to be in the vanguard of the advance of the "East."[3] A process that took centuries in Europe is to be carried through in as many decades. Here again there is evinced the new sense of vitality, the new tempo of life.

The manifold nationalities of the Soviet Union, which is distinguished from the Tsarist empire by the absence from its territory of the peoples most under western influence, the Poles and Finns, add to the supra-Russian significance of the social and cultural policy of the Union. There is no uniformity of cultural and economic development within the Soviet Union; in relation to the other nationalities, especially the people of its eastern borders, the Russian people has played the part of the more advanced people, "exploiting" the others as "colonial" populations. Consequently the nationality policy of the Soviet Union becomes in its turn a facet of the world-wide settling of accounts between "East" and "West," an element in the transition to another stage of history. It takes up on a different plane and treats with new methods an old problem of Imperialism, the problem of the incorporation of numerous peoples of varied levels of culture and economic development in a unified political organization and a single economic body. This policy is no longer being carried out by the capitalist society of traders and investors, saturated as that often is with the remains of the old feudal order, and by "intellectuals" born in and attached to that society, but by new, "barbaric" social classes, summoned now from the apathy of the times when men took no thought for the future, to play their part in history for the first time, adapting to their purpose western methods of production and organization, and guided by a faith born of western philosophy.

THE PILLARS OF THE NEW ORDER

My nash, my novy mir postroyem:
Kto byl nitchem, tot stanet vsem.

(We are building our world, the new world:
And he who was nothing will be everything.)

> Russian text of the "Internationale."

But before you can think so clearly you must have suffered, the old world must have died within you. If you do not curse the old world with your whole heart, ay, from the depths of your heart, you are not yet ripe for the new world. . . .

Now the workshop has begun thundering away. That was plain language that the hammers spoke! How much did the reverend gentleman's soft words count againt that?

> HEINRICH LERSCH: *Hammerschläge.*

The dominant ideas of an age have always been simply those of the dominant class. The Communist Revolution is the most radical breakaway from the traditional property conditions; no wonder that in the course of its development the most radical break is made with the traditional ideas.

> MARX and ENGELS, in the *Communist Manifesto.*

Up to the coming of the Revolution, the condi
tions in the Russian Empire had militated against
the development of any national consciousness
in the modern sense. The gulf between the
various classes and social strata had been much
too wide; the masses had had no share in the
wealth of the highly peculiar and charming
culture of the intelligentzia, and had had no
access to it. State and society were two strongly
contrasted things, as in Central Europe before
1848. The political mysticism of the ruling
class, both in its revolutionary and westernized
and in its Slavophil and reactionary elements,
had no contact with the real life of the masses
and could not carry them with it. And there
was no sense of alien domination such as,
under similar circumstances, might have brought
a nationalist movement into being. The Russian
revolutions of the twentieth century for the first
time brought the masses into activity, inspired
them with a political mysticism, and provided
through democratization the conditions for a
nationalist movement. But the movement had
scarcely taken shape when its content changed
from nationalism to Communism. It was the
lack of a true sense of nationhood, of any cultural

bond between all classes in common cultural traditions and ideals, that made it possible for the Communist Revolution completely to disperse in Russia the minute section of society that had upheld the old culture, and within a brief period to form a new human type as upholder of the new order.

The other nationalities of the Russian realm, which had been as wholly untouched by modern life as the Russian masses, were associated with them by the new rulers in the support of the new state. No more than two generations ago the mass of the population of the Russian Empire were still serfs. In recent years the masses have provided from their midst a "vanguard"—youth and the proletariat. These form the new society, this time identical with the state; they create its new standards of social and intellectual life, and communicate the pulse of its life to the masses. These new "barbaric" elements now rule in the Soviet Union, and not only rule but inspire it with their own vitality, determine its manner of living, and set the standards of value. The Soviet Union is the worker's, the proletarian's state,[4] conceptually and constitutionally; it not only accords him the leading positions in the state and in economic life, it not only appropriates the higher educational institutions primarily to his service, but it also endeavours, as the middle classes did before it, to form the whole community in his image. In this lies the deeper significance of the revolution which has been in progress since 1928 in the country-side of the Soviet Union, aiming at the conversion of the peasants into proletarians. With the introduction into the country-side of machinery and of the types of works and of organization customary in urban and industrial life, the distinction between town and country is to disappear, and with it the traditional narrowly rural and slow-going character of the peasant.[5] In place of the old individualistic farming methods there now comes the collectivist grain mill with its minute division of labour, its great capital expenditure on plant and equipment, and the opportunity it affords for carrying urban culture and the urban type of organization into the country-side. The conversion of schools into polytechnics introduces the children from their earliest years to the tasks and the outlook of the proletariat, draws them into the great working process, makes them a part of a factory or collective enterprise.

The proletariat, born of the machine and of modern industrial methods, sees in the machine and in industry the means of all progress.

Thus the new youth of the Soviet Union comes from social strata that until now had had no contact with and no part in the old culture. In its rationalistic outlook and its determination to get things done it has nothing in common with the young intellectuals of pre-revolutionary Russia. In the issue between Hegelianism, the belief in the possibility of a rational interpretation of history, in the adequacy and ability of reason to comprehend the historic process and interpret its enigmas, and the philosophy of Schopenhauer, the belief in dark irrational forces as the ultimate determinants of human life, in the meaninglessness of history, from which only the individual can escape into Nirvana, not the collectivity, Soviet youth has cast its vote for Hegel. Human reason, it holds, acquires creativeness through its recognition and furtherance of the process which reveals itself in history; in the confidence in this there lies a challenge to human will-power. This Soviet youth is suffused with a new stamina and decision. In the world of the proletariat labour is elevated to the creative principle. In the precapitalist world labour was a curse or an inescapable evil; in the capitalist world it was rehabilitated, was justified by its results even to the length of the American attitude that took the level of a man's income as the outward and visible measure of God's blessing. So the estimation of money was pitched higher and higher until in America it became the supreme measure of value. In Communism the dignity of labour comes once more into its own, and the social estimation of the individual is made entirely independent of his income. With the worker as the highest in the land, labour gains a new ennoblement.[6] Over Moscow there floats the flaming device: "We shall point a new way for the world; labour shall become lord of the world." Confidence in themselves as a new conquering class, youthful naïveté and joy in pioneering, and the relish of the machine and the untold wealth that it yields, inspire the youth of the Soviet Union to deeds of which the meaning and purpose are fixed in advance by the philosophic system which has become their faith, and lead them to break with a religion built up on man's humility in the face of the incomprehensible and his recognition of the limitedness of his powers. The new youth are full of contempt and incomprehension of an outlook which does not regard the immanence of human reason as the supereminent source of the energies of human life and of man's history.   In their view "Science has killed God."   They have not hesitated, thus far, to be "as gods, knowing good and evil."

This rationalized religion, concerned only with the world we live in, this religion of socialized life and labour, was bound to come into conflict with the traditional religions which had pronounced the sacredness of private property.   It did not have any stubbornly fought contest.[7] The Russian church had no deep roots in the soul of the Russian.   It had venerable and ancient dignity, but was encrusted with a pomp and formalism beneath which there was no spiritual life, no social activity and no concern for the problems and needs of the time.   It had never heard the call of the age, had had no guidance to offer amid the spiritual and social needs of the changing Russia, and had felt no responsibility in regard to them.   Nor did it stand aloof from things temporal in order to preach the eternal living word of God.   It had placed its whole existence at the service of a social system and a system of living of which the days were already numbered, a system which had long been decaying from within; and it could not survive the system. Thus the efforts to put new life into the dead bones when difficult times came, and to found a "Living Church," were foredoomed to failure. It was not the "propaganda of the godless"[8] but the ardent faith of the Soviet youth that won the day against the old churches. Religion to the Soviet youth was "Opium for the People," no awakening of creative initiative and of the energies of the masses for the conversion of this earth into the Kingdom of God, but a reconciling of the masses to their miserable conditions of existence by means of a promised future life, so leaving the rich and the powerful to the undisturbed enjoyment of the ordering of this world in their service. Instead of humble acceptance of the state into which it should please God to call them, the disinherited of this earth were now to be invested with their heritage by the exercise of their own will and pleasure.

The Communists set out, however, to do battle for the soul of man on a still more fundamental plane. Religion is the overcoming of fear, of the fear that the finite human being feels for the

c

infinity around him. The human life with its
narrow limits in time and space is constrained to
rise above and beyond itself, it seeks refuge and
safety, strength and endurance in the eternal
and absolute, to which it is prepared to sacrifice
itself in order to enter into eternal life. Lenin
gave a new interpretation to this creaturely fear
in the age of Capitalism. The liability of Capitalism to crises, and the dependence on far-away
events over which there can be no control, rob
the worker and the peasant of to-day of all
security of existence. They are menaced at all
times by the ghastly spectre of unemployment
and starvation—a blind and incalculable peril
before which, in the capitalist economic order,
they are helpless. The planned economic system
of Socialism will relieve the masses of the fear
for their livelihood.

But this economic fear for his livelihood is not
man's only mortal fear. His creaturely fear
proceeds from more fundamental depths in the
human soul. In modern times the religious
conception of the world with its sheltering God
had broken down. The individual had become
master of himself, and at home amid his natural
world and the laws which it observed, but no

longer felt assured of the continuance of his existence in any purely transcendental sense. Under the stress of his isolation he sought for association, for permanence, for immortality: for a bond, for "religion." Here we have the basis of the significance of nationalism as the religious force of modern times. In community with his compatriots, with whom he forms a living and organic whole, the individual finds companionship on his way and a removal of the limitations of his influence; it is thus in our times that he attains an extension and multiplication of his personality amid the national mass-emotions, as the individual of the past did amid the ecstasies of worship. In the deeps of succeeding ages, in the historic chain of contacts reaching from his first ancestors in the beginning of time through his descendants into the far future, he finds a guarantee of his permanence, heirs of his will, an immortality that, in Fichte's phrase, "interlaces the heavenly in the earthly"—an eternity in the concrete permanence of the bloodstream of earthly generations. The fear that besets the individual is now stilled in the continuity of the nation, to which he is ready to sacrifice himself in order to save his eternal life. In place of responsibility before God there comes responsibility before the generations to come.

The capitalist economic order which developed in the age of nationalism brought a period of growth and prosperity precisely to the nations that were most advanced in national consciousness, and at the same time in industrialization; it brought a prosperity in which the masses shared, and a comparative security from economic want. Since the dissolution of the religious orders of the middle ages, nationalism has been the main pillar of the faith of the men of the new age. But whereas in God, as the absolute transcendental conception, there exist the elements of the œcumene or universal order, he being the creator of all things finite and the father of all men, the principle of nationalism is a dissolution of the œcumene. In the early capitalist period economic life was organized in the national areas which, through their association with the populations that they contained, became the units of the history of the new age. To-day the spatial opportunities and requirements of trade have outgrown these limits. In the epoch of advanced traffic development and world trade the economic existence of the individual and its needs, the satisfaction of which is only thinkable in the œcumene, have become separated from the spiritual existence, which still imagines itself assured in the nationalism that is destructive of every œcumene. Communism, which seeks to anchor the spiritual existence of man in a new faith, to liberate him from his fear and insecurity through a new shelteredness, is turning back to the œcumene. But by the very process of dragging the peoples of the Soviet Union out of the period of religious mediævalism through its work of enlightenment, and leading them to a new trust in themselves and to modern technical production, it awakens in them also the will to self-expression and to cohesion of the nation, and there grows up in them, not through the traditional religions but through nationalism, the opposing force with which Communism has to contend not only in the Russian people but in the other peoples inhabiting the Soviet Union.

The particular character of the nationalism which developed in the age of individualism gave it in its early formative period the faculty of understanding and tolerance. The roots of nationalism reach down into the solid ground of eighteenth-century Liberalism and of the intellectual breadth of rationalism. Such nationally-minded spirits as Herder were interested in the popular arts and the characteristics of all other peoples. Nationalists of one country were enthusiastic for the national freedom of other peoples. Every nation had its own way to salvation, stressed for the very reason of its own peculiar character the peculiar character of other peoples, and consented to their pursuit of independent courses. Not until organized nations came into conflict did nationalism acquire its destructive intolerance. Regarded, however, from the standpoint of the œcumene, it remained individualistic. This was in strong contrast to the attitude of the mediæval œcumenical religions, whose roads to salvation had, in principle, been binding on and open to all men. They claimed a monopoly of validity. But for that very reason they had an implicit tendency to unity. The system of political nationalism always assumes the existence of various nations in their states alongside one another; the Church and Communism aim in their systems at a single all-embracing society, united in faith in the one case, classless in the other. Under the national system there still remains a struggle between nations; œcumenical religion and Communism point the way through their fulfilment to an age of universalism and peace.   In this, too, Communism is a return to the faith of the men of the middle ages.

THE NEW FAITH

If any man come to me, and hate not his father, and mother, and wife, and children, and brethren, and sisters, yea, and his own life also, he cannot be my disciple.

Luke xiv, 26.

And if thy right eye offend thee, pluck it out, and cast it from thee: for it is profitable for thee that one of thy members should perish, and not that thy whole body should be cast into hell.

Matthew v, 29.

And he said unto them, Thus saith the Lord God of Israel, Put every man his sword by his side, and go in and out from gate to gate throughout the camp, and slay every man his brother, and every man his companion, and every man his neighbour.

And the children of Levi did according to the word of Moses: and there fell of the people that day about three thousand men.

For Moses had said, Consecrate yourselves to-day to the Lord, even every man upon his son, and upon his brother; that He may bestow upon you a blessing this day.

Exodus xxxii, 27–29.

(After the dance around the golden calf.)

THE philosophic roots of the Communist intellectual system, which explains every historical, social, and spiritual happening on the Hegelian principle, and rests the hope of salvation on the obedience to law of the historic process of which it is the culmination, lie in the nineteenth century. The Communist intellectual system is irradiated by the conviction that the world is controlled and ordered through the growth of the rationalist spirit, a growth immanent in the world. The comprehensiveness and completeness of this system give it a solidity which assigns it to a different plane of existence from that of mere social philosophy. Anyone who has assimilated and accepts this system possesses the key to the explanation of all things and the assured knowledge of the path to be pursued in the future. Beneath and alongside this system there may be deeps out of which primordial sources of life burst forth, but it is unnecessary for this to be taken account of by those who build on this system as bedrock—until the floods from those deeps burst their bonds and surge around it.

The religious glow and uncompromising nature of Communism lift it out of the relativity of its philosophical origins. It asserts the same claim to absoluteness as mediæval faith. The outlook on life of the masses who have adopted it has nothing in common with Europe. For the European and Western way of thought, as distinguished from that of the rest of the world, is the product of the Renaissance and the Reformation, and above all of the age of rationalism. These have built up the humanism on the basis of which scepticism has been accepted as a legitimate intellectual attitude, and critical consideration as an indefeasible right of the individual. Only such a scepticism, prepared to admit that alongside one's own path to truth there may be others, that the absolute is only made manifest in various relative interpretations, each of which has an equal right to be put forward, can permit liberty of thought and opinion, can practise tolerance and form a basis for the growth of individualism. What Europe has won thus in breadth and freedom, it has lost in certainty. Anyone who does not believe that there is only one road to the salvation of mankind, and that one his own, is easily led into compromises, is able to respect the liberty of his fellow-man, is preserved from the peril of ὕβρις, of being ready, like

Ibsen's Brand, to sacrifice every natural bond to his god. The fanaticism of the Communists springs from their un-European type of faith, with its mediæval absoluteness.

That type of faith is also to be observed in the central position in Communist thought taken by the works of Marx and Lenin, a position which gives those works the rank of sacred writings. Proof from chapter and verse, the support of a contention by quotations from Marx and Lenin, clinches the argument as in all mediæval religions; the exegesis of the sacred writings and the appeal to them forms the centre of discussion. The lack of freedom, the "intolerance" and "inhumanity" of Communism similarly find their explanation in its mediæval type of faith. It demands men's full and entire adhesion, allowing no validity to any other ties of nature or choice—as in the blessing which Moses pronounced on Levi:*

"Who said unto his father and to his mother, I have not seen him; neither did he acknowledge his brethren, nor knew his own children: for they

---

* Deuteronomy xxxiii, 9. The German text runs : "Wer *von* seinem Vater und seiner Mutter spricht."—"He who says of his father and of his mother, I do not see him, and of his brother, I do not know him, and of his son, I know not—these observe thy word, and keep thy covenant."—Translator.

have observed thy word, and kept thy covenant,"
and in the words of Jesus:

"For I am come to set a man at variance against
his father, and the daughter against her mother.
. . . He that loveth father or mother more than
me is not worthy of me; and he that loveth son or
daughter more than me is not worthy of me."

The Communist Party is in spirit "a kingdom
of priests."[9]

Similarly the position of art and science under
Communism is mediæval. They are not their
own justification, they are not the legitimate
expression of the creative passion of the individual;
they serve the building up of Socialism, the
glorification of the faith and its justification
through works. They have to fit themselves
into a general scheme which demands the whole
of a man and allows no private sphere. Art
strives, too, in the Soviet Union after the anonymity which characterized the Gothic cathedrals
and mediæval sculpture. The craftsman and the
creator retire behind their work; and their work
takes its place as one stone in the building which is
to be the foundation of the new human race that
is to come. Artists and experts are brethren in a
builders' hut, united in building up through

faith and the spirit of service. Each one does no more than fulfil his function in this highly-departmentalized work of construction, and counts only in so far as he fulfils this function. Modern individualism, with its emphasis on the independent value of the individual, has no place here; biography loses all interest, only service counts.[10]

This religion, like every mediæval or pre-rationalistic religion, divides humanity sharply into believers and unbelievers. The moral conceptions of rationalism have no validity here. As in Calvinism, works count for nothing; belief counts for nothing; only election—though in Calvinism the election of men to grace is entirely passive, whereas in Communism man has actively to seize hold of the saving truth. The consciousness of this saving truth gives the Communists their assurance and positiveness: the opponent is always wrong, for he is the supporter of the enemy of the true ordering of things; the Communist is always right, for he is contending for God's world. There can be no compromise here: He who is not with me is against me. Neutrality and objectivity, a cautious weighing of issues under the promptings of conscience or

of the knowledge of the processes of life and of
history, are not admitted. Anyone who "sits
on the fence" in any way is a noxious pest who
must be cleared from the path. In this secularized
gospel the hardness that shrinks from nothing is
the true service to the attainment of the goal, to
the liberation of humanity from sufferings that
have continued for thousands of years. Only the
goal matters, the individual rights of each human
life, of each generation are ruthlessly sacrificed
to it. The eschatological element in Communism,
according to which the goal is to be attained
within measurable time—the goal of a classless
and forceless society living in brotherly harmony
and lasting peace, of the union of all men in
common creative work for the mastery of Nature,
the taming of all dark and menacing forces, and
the removal of all suffering and all bodily and
spiritual want—banishes entirely the static element of religious salvation, the association of
every individual soul and every concrete situation
with the absolute, in favour of the dynamic
element. The forty years' wandering through
the wilderness has begun, and the generation
that has entered the wilderness must die before the
Promised Land is reached.

But will not the sacrifice of every static element to the dynamic of the goal, the consecration of all means by the end, this exclusive concern with the future, endanger the goal itself? The Communist's certainty of victory is not based on ethical superiority but on a confidence free from all moral context, based, as Engels wrote, on the material consideration of the fact "that there must be a revolution in the method of production and distribution which sets aside all differences of class, if the whole of modern society is not to suffer dissolution. On this tangible material fact, which is forcing its way irresistibly into the heads of the exploited proletarians in more or less clear shape, on this fact and not on the conceptions of right and wrong of this or the other arm-chair theoretician, is based the certainty of victory of modern Socialism."

With this mediæval attitude of faith is combined the faith in progress of the nineteenth century. Its instruments remain the same—the natural and social sciences, technical and engineering progress, statistics and psychology. But the faith in progress itself undergoes a characteristic transformation. The idea of progress, born of the old Jewish religious concept of human history as one process directed by one divine will towards one end, was secularized in the eighteenth century, but only became the universal basis of existence in the nineteenth century. Not only was the actual tempo of development immensely quicker than in any earlier times, but the attitude to it had altered. In spite of steady but slow change, past centuries had been essentially periods of rest; the nineteenth century was the first that was conscious of this steady change. Its unceasing progress was filled with a restless, forward-urging zeal for change; but this was progress in general, without a definite goal, unplanned, and limitless in its course. Communism has dammed up this progress in the stream-bed of systematic planning, has given it a near and definite goal in place of the course into the unknown, has pulled it down from the stars and planted it on earth. This gives time and its measurement in relation to the goal a new and increased significance. Time is plainly linked up once more, as in the middle ages, from a beginning (the fall of man, through the organization of class dominance by means of the state) through a revealed gospel (the doctrine of Socialism concerning the meaning of history) to the final age (the classless society). Progress, formerly a vague belief reinforced by experience, becomes the foundation on which everything rests. The proletariat is the bearer, predetermined by the whole course of history, of the impending world revolution. But what is at issue is not the interests of the proletariat or of any section of humanity, but the single and indivisible interest of humanity as a whole.

Thus in the idea of progress, Communism outbids the nineteenth century; it does so also in its missionary purpose, which fills it with a fervour which once distinguished Christendom and Islam.[11] The welding together of the peoples of the earth in one great society, which Capitalism began, has been continued by Communism in a much more deliberate way and in the radically different spirit of an equal partnership of all peoples, advanced and backward, white and coloured, in all of which, irrespectively of all national divisions, there are upholders and forerunners of the new order, and their enemies.[12] In the picture which Communism paints of the approaching realm of peace it adopts once more an old religious conception; and it does so also in the fact that it expects no individual salvation but only a

D

universal one, since the life of all men and all peoples, in appearance isolated and subject to interests of their own, is in reality only a part of the unity of the history of society.

Thus for Communism all that counts is the horizontal link in humanity, the class, spread over the whole world, which is not bound up with the formative forces of historical tradition, or fed with the nourishing juices of a property of its own, deeply rooted in the soil of a definite parcel of the earth's surface. In this attitude it is irreconcilably opposed to the nationalism for which it is the vertical link that determines the course of history—the society that embraces all classes, that raises itself on a definitely delimited territorial area and, carrying with it the memory of past generations, takes deep root in its soil. Nationalism, such as it is especially in its early stages, is capable of being democratic, in the sense of the phrase "Make the people's cause the nation's, and then the nation's cause will be the people's," and of assuming solidarity with the interests of the masses; but the ultimate political value, the association that decides destinies, lies for it in the nation. In this it takes up its position entirely in the historic period that extended from the eighteenth century to the world war. The latest manifestations of nationalism, Fascism and National Socialism—the roots of which lie partly in the romantic period of early nationalism and partly in the ambition to "get a move on" of the men of the beginning of the twentieth century, in their longing for a life of activity and heroism—have much that has a superficial resemblance to Communism and much that is a perversion of it, but have nothing whatever in common with it. They belong to the nationalist century that still lives on; Communism belongs to a new stage of history. Their revolutions are thus *coups d'état* that make no change in the basic structure of society; the Communist revolution, on the contrary, effects a fundamental change conceived at the outset for the whole world. Communism no longer sees in the nation and the national state the life-giving force, the determinant of the course of history, the turning-point in the historic struggle; for Communism it is membership of a class that provides the formative force, that makes history, with its suffering and despair out of which ultimately come liberation and salvation. There is no room for the dark forces of race in its awakening to conscious endeavour. But in the arena of its efforts at fulfilment Communism has inevitably come again and again into conflict with nationalism and its forces, has had to try to find a *modus vivendi* with them, to fit them into their place, and so to dispose of them.

BOLSHEVISM AND NATIONALISM: THE SITUATION AND THE PLAN OF ACTION

> In a word, the Communists support everywhere every revolutionary movement against the existing social and political conditions.
>
> MARX and ENGELS: *The Communist Manifesto*.

> The national question is a part of the general question of the proletarian revolution, a part of the question of proletarian dictatorship . . . a part that is subordinate in relation to the whole and must be considered and treated from the point of view of the whole. . . . The concrete historic conditions as starting-point, logical deduction from them as the only right method—that is the key to the solution of the question of nationality.
>
> STALIN.

WHEN the Russian Empire collapsed in 1917, it left to Communism an evil heritage in the national sphere; though it was inhabited by many nationalities and several religious communities, it acknowledged only one dominating nation and only one official religion of the empire. The other peoples of the empire had no national rights, and many of them, such as the Jews and the *Inorodtzi* ("aliens by origin"), as the non-Russian populations in Asia and along the Volga were officially termed, had no civil rights. Russian was the only official language, the only language of the courts of justice and the government schools and the administration. Yet the Russians formed only 43 per cent of the population, though official statistics managed to contrive a Russian majority of 63 per cent by counting in the Ukrainians and the White Russians. There were no limits to the state policy of the Russification of all the non-Russian populations and their conversion to the Orthodox church. The schools founded or assisted by the state were conducted solely for the benefit of the Russian population or for the furtherance of Russification. The other peoples were not permitted the use of their language in public business, and were allowed no opportunities of cultivating and developing it. There were no government schools carried on for them in their mother tongue. The position of privilege of the Russian element in all things political, cultural, and economic was steadily maintained

in every possible way. Nothing was done for the
cultural and economic progress of the non-
Russian populations, least of all for the Inorodtzi.
State and church rivalled one another in a ruthless
policy of colonization; the best lands were taken
away from the autochthonous owners and
distributed among Russian colonists.

Russification was carried on with especial harsh-
ness among the Slav peoples allied to the Russians
in race and language. There was no recognition
whatever of the Ukrainian and White Russian
nationalities. Until 1905 it was forbidden even
for books and newspapers to be printed in
Ukrainian, White Russian, or Lithuanian. The
nationalist movements which began in the nineteenth century among the most progressive of
these peoples were driven, in the interests of their
own nationhood, and its freedom of development,
to work for a complete change in the Russian
system of government and, accordingly, to ally
themselves with the liberalizing revolutionary
movement among the Russian intelligentzia.

This parallelism between the revolutionary
and the nationalist movements—which, for all
that, often had to fight out radical differences of
aim, since the Russian revolutionaries, and

even many of the Socialists, were themselves
nationalistically-minded Russians and held fast
to the ideas of the unity of the Russian realm
and the predominance of the Russian element—
showed itself plainly in the 1905 revolution. In
those months of 1905 the propagandists of the
revolution carried into the most distant parts of
the empire the slogans of liberty and self-determination, summoned the masses of the peasantry,
and also the backward peoples, to participation
in public life, and were a powerful influence in
the awakening of the national consciousness of
peoples which until then had been sunk in
lethargy. Alongside the general awakening of
nationalism among the Mohammedan peoples
and in Asia in the first decade of the twentieth
century, there developed a parallel movement
among the eastern peoples inhabiting the Russian
Empire. The Constitution of October 1905
wrung from the state by the revolution brought
some relief to the population of the Russian
Empire on the national plane as elsewhere; but
scarcely had the autocracy regained a sense
of security when an amendment of the Constitution (June 1907) robbed the border territories
inhabited by non-Russian peoples of their repre-

sentation. Once, however, the popular sense of
nationhood had been awakened by the revolutionary movement of 1905, it never died out.

Russian chauvinism continually fed the flame
of nationalism among the oppressed peoples.
The fact that even the Left wing of the Russian
intelligentzia was unprepared to renounce the
many advantages which accrued from the use
of the Russian language alone as the official
language of the empire, and from the placing of
the machinery of the state in the service of the
dominance of the Russian tongue and the Russian
element in all branches of public life, intensified
the friction between the national groups. The
Turkish revolution of 1908 and Turco-Turanian
nationalism found a lively echo among the
Turco-Tartar peoples of the Tsarist empire.
The world war with its slogans of national self-
determination and its awakening of public interest
in national affairs brought into sharp relief the
incompatibilities between the Russian and the
other peoples of the empire. Not a few of the
latter saw their national independence within
sight; among the Russian intelligentzia, in their
turn, the war had infused fresh life into the idea
of the Russian Empire—they dreamed of a new

strengthening of Russia's and their own power and influence, and even far to the Left among the intelligentzia there was no readiness to show practical sympathy with the efforts of the other nationalities to achieve their enfranchisement, at the cost of the restriction of the centralised power of the Russian state and the predominance of the Russian element. The conflict which threatened to come between the revolutionary and nationalist liberation movements could only be averted through a supra-national outlook; the only way in which there could be any hope of bringing to an end the clash of vital and irrational forces of race and nationality was through the recognition of the force of a rational and supra-national ordering of social life. In this situation Lenin proclaimed the right of the peoples of the Russian Empire to complete self-determination, even to secession from the empire. With the putting into practice of that slogan the historic and national Russian realm ceased to exist (although the two formative forces of its history, the geographical laws of its territorial extent and the characteristic mentality of its nationality, continued to operate); its successor claimed to belong to a new supra-national order.

Lenin had been occupying himself with the question of nationality long before the world war. In such a structure as the Russian Empire, that threatened ultimately to fly into fragments through its internal national tensions, tensions which were a standing hindrance to the solution of social and cultural problems, the attention of the Socialists, who regarded it as their mission to secure the economic and cultural advance of the masses, was bound to be turned, as in Austria, to the problem of nationality. The Austrian Social Democrats were unable to find a solution for the nationality problem even to the satisfaction of their own membership; their leading theoreticians had no more effectual solution to offer than that of national cultural autonomy. Lenin went far beyond the Austrian Marxists. For him the question of nationality had no independent existence; it was a subsidiary problem of the social revolution, and could not be dealt with in isolation from the questions of the domination of capital, the fight against Imperialism, and the proletarian dictatorship. It was within this complex of questions that a solution had to be found for the question of nationality, for the sake of the wider aim of the liberation of the oppressed masses of all nations. In his championship of the right of all peoples to complete self-determination he had no idea of dividing up the surface of the earth and the field it offered to the economic and social activity of man into a multiplicity of rigidly isolated states. His goal was the rapprochement of the peoples and their fusion into associations and economic units of the maximum dimensions, even of world-wide dimensions. But he was aware that this rapprochement could only be effected on the basis of the freedom and the voluntary adhesion of the various peoples. The slightest oppression of one people by another, any privilege of nationality or tongue, any identification of the state or empire with the interests of a particular nation as wielder of the authority of the state or empire, was bound to arouse opposition among the peoples or offshoots of peoples thereby placed at a disadvantage, to kindle a combative nationalism, and to wreck the one condition essential to fraternal collaboration and mutual support between the workers of all peoples in the building up of a new social order. Lenin, with his keen sense of the necessity of a policy based on a thorough grasp of realities and a full weighing of them, resisted every attempt to belittle the national question from an "international" point of view. He always pointed out that it was of the utmost importance to appreciate the full gravity of the nationality problem, and to search for a solution, if it was desired to divest it of its gravity and rob it of its sting in the future. Thus, in the question of nationalism as elsewhere, Lenin chose the analysis of the actual facts as his point of departure and the dialectical inference from the facts as his method.

Even before the Revolution Lenin did not content himself with general slogans of autonomy, but defined quite clearly the task of the Socialists in the nationalist movement. The Socialists among the ruling or privileged people had a different task from that of Socialists among oppressed peoples. The Socialists of the dominant people were to stand for the abrogation of all national privileges and for the oppressed peoples' right of secession from the state or empire. In every step they took they were to have regard to the sensitiveness of the oppressed peoples on national issues. The Socialists among the oppressed people were to proclaim the identity of the interests of the proletariat of their own people with those of the proletariat among the oppressing people, and to combat the misuse of national slogans by the dominant classes of their own people. Thus in the nationality question the Socialists had, under Capitalism, to "swim against the stream."

But the nationality question did not cease to exist for Lenin with the ending of the capitalist order. It would retain its significance, he held, for a long time under the dictatorship of the proletariat, until the proletarian policy had succeeded in extirpating the peoples' hatred and mistrust of one another—until the great differences in civilization and in standard of living between the dominant and subject peoples had been wiped out by education and economic policy, and the masses had been invested with the spirit of internationalism and of fraternal neighbourliness between the peoples.

Lenin saw no unalterable force, ineradicable from human nature, in nationalism; he saw in the nation no god-given ordering of human existence, ordained for all time. He realized that in its historic associations the nation is the product of a definite stage in history. In his view the bourgeois era was also the era of the development of nationalism. The birth of Capi-

talism and of nationalism originally signified a
liberation of creative forces, an upward step in
historic development. But as Capitalism developed, its liberating tendency ultimately turned
into the opposite. "In its battle with feudalism,"
Lenin wrote, "Capitalism had been a liberator of
nations; but imperialistic Capitalism (the Capitalism of recent times) became the greatest of
oppressors of nations." With the destruction of
Capitalism and of national oppression, with the
achievement of the full equality of all peoples,
political nationalism will disappear. Economic
progress, the pressure of which in the beginnings
of Capitalism produced the amalgamation of tribes
and provinces into nations through the need for
larger economic units, is now applying pressure
through the process of the solution of the crises
which are shaking Capitalism, through the transition from Capitalism to Socialism, in the direction
of more and more comprehensive territorial
amalgamations. Thus, with the achievement of
Socialism nationalism will gradually disappear
and the nationality question will steadily lose
importance. It is just in order that this final
goal may be reached, and not for its own sake,
that at the present time nationalism must be

recognized as a factor and taken into account. This recognition will give nationalism a relative character, in place of the absolute character which it had during the last century and a half, as a final goal of political, social, and cultural activity, a fulfilment of nationhood for its own sake, for the sake of its sublimity and its historic mission. Nationalism will become a means to a higher end, will be judged by its appropriateness to that end, and will be given its place in the unified complex of the coming humanity, a complex which it threatened in its absolute form to hamper or even to rend asunder. Such was Lenin's argument.

After the seizure of power in the autumn of 1917, Lenin lost no time in tackling the nationality problem, as one of the first that called for attention, on the lines indicated in his slogans. Stalin, a Georgian from Transcaucasia, the typical country of embittered national struggles, became his principal collaborator in this work. The Socialist groups in Stalin's country had always placed the problem of their nation in the fore-front of their theoretical discussion and their practical policy. Many of them had seen in the national struggle for liberation the central purpose of their activity. Stalin had defended the proletarian standpoint of Marxism against them before the world war. As early as 1912 he had written a pamphlet on Marxism and the question of nationality, in which he had devoted especial attention to countering the theory of individual national autonomy as put forward by the Austrian Social Democrats. After the Revolution Stalin became the head of the People's Commissariat for nationality questions. In that post he laid down the principles on which the Communist nationality policy was carried into effect. At the tenth and twelfth Communist Party congresses, in which the nationality question was discussed in its fundamental and tactical aspects, Stalin opened the discussion as *rapporteur*. And as Lenin's heir he steadily maintained the course of the nationality policy of the Soviet Union from the moment when it was first announced in the Declaration of the Rights of the Peoples of Russia on November 15, 1917.

This Declaration laid down the following basic principles: Equality and sovereignty of the peoples of Russia, their right to full self-determination, including secession from Russia and setting up as independent states; the abrogation

E

of all privileges and disabilities of nationalities and national religions; freedom of development of national minorities and ethnical groups in Russian territory. The French Revolution, which had been the herald of national awakening and individualization in Europe, had contented itself with the proclamation of the individual's right to freedom. The Russian Revolution, setting the seal on the historic progress of the hundred and twenty years that had passed since then, had added to the rights of the individual citizen the rights of peoples. The significance of the collective individualities which are represented through nationhood had secured recognition, the "national era" had opened out into full bloom and had spread, under the influence of the two Russian revolutions themselves, to the remotest regions of the East. No attempt at a solution of the social troubles of the time could any longer ignore the nationality problem.

Nor could it evade it by using a new formula, not based on the actual conditions, to anticipate a desired situation. A "Left" internationalist group, under the leadership of Bukharin, tried to do this at the eighth Communist Party Congress, demanding the rejection of the rights of self-

determination and of secession for the nationalities led by bourgeois elements or consisting of
them, and proposing to recognize a right of
self-determination only for the working masses of
the various peoples. In his reply Lenin drew
attention to the realities of the case, to the social
facts that had come to fruition in the course of
history: "To refuse to recognize the Thing that
Is, cannot be permitted: recognition enforces
itself." Interference by another people, and
especially by one which had the superiority in
numbers or culture or industry, could only
hinder or hold up the process of class differentiation in the nationalist movement of a politically
weaker people and reinforce the hold of
nationalism over the masses.

Thus Leninism took account of the national
groups as social factors; but the Communists,
in their belief in the fundamental uniformity of
human nature and its susceptibility to influence
through education and social conditions of existence, could not recognize as of all-dominating
absoluteness the claims of the organic units
resulting from blood-relationship and common
history; they could not accept the passionate
struggle of nations for self-preservation and for

the extension of their power, the tragedy of the collision between national rights and energies, unrestrained by any purely rational considerations. They drew from their own faith the confidence in their ability to master in the new order the struggle between the dark national instincts and the chaos that springs from it.

With the seizure of power, the problem of nationality gained for Lenin a wider scope. Hitherto it had been a constitutional problem affecting Russian home affairs; it now presented itself, from the point of view of the world revolution, on a world-wide scale. The dynamic energy of the oppressed nations, especially of colonial peoples, had now to be harnessed to the service of the Revolution. The slogan "Proletarians of the world, unite," was expanded into "Proletarians of all countries and oppressed peoples of all the world, unite." The Declaration of the Rights of the Peoples of Russia was followed a few days later by a proclamation addressed to the Mohammedan workers of Russia and the East, calling on them to organize their national life in entire freedom, and assuring them of the assistance of the Russian proletariat. So it was that the attention of the Soviet Government was turned to the nationality problem of the East.

Here the Soviet Union followed the same course that it had taken in the economic and social transformation of the East, in its industrialization and in the awakening of its masses: it took up its position in the front rank of the political struggle for the liberation of the colonial and quasi-colonial peoples. It took up the struggle all along the line with Imperialism, the late phase of Capitalism. The capitalist Powers needed economic and political colonies. Through the economic and political emancipation of these colonies Lenin hoped to be able to strike staggering blows at Imperialism. The social condition and the state of education of the masses in the eastern countries were not dissimilar to those of the Tsarist empire, but the element of national oppression further reinforced the revolutionary potentialities. The eastern peoples' newly awakened sense of their own dignity made them specially sensitive to manifestations of the Westerner's sense of superiority.

The Soviet Union made a clean break with the traditional conceptions of the relations between East and West. In the very first days of its existence it renounced in one great gesture all priorities and capitulations, concessions, and privileges, which the Tsarist Government had possessed in Asiàtic countries in common with all other European Powers and with the United States. In the treaties which the Soviet Union concluded with these Asiatic states, they were recognized and treated for the first time in their existence as complete equals; their efforts to secure their sovereignty and freedom were for the first time expressly welcomed.[13] This attitude on the part of the Soviet Union made it easier for Turkey and Persia after the world war to achieve full independence, and to make an end of the foreigners' position of privilege in their territories. Sun Yat-sen, the father of Chinese nationalism, saw in an alliance with the Soviet Union China's road to liberation from the Imperialism of the Powers. After Sun Yat-sen's death the assistance of the Soviet Union enabled his nationalist party, the Kuomintang, to unite China.

Communist propaganda failed, however, to consolidate its successes in the countries of the East. The native propertied classes shrank from the dangers of a social revolution and the chaos which it would bring in its train. They watered down the revolutionary national demands and plans of reform, and evinced readiness to come to terms with the imperialist Powers. The prospects of Communist propaganda in the East can only increase if the pressure exerted by foreign Imperialism increases, and the economic distress of the masses, especially the peasants, is accentuated.

But even without Communist propaganda, the rapid growth of the nationalist movement in Asia in the coming years may inflict yet more formidable blows on the economic and political position of Imperialism than have been delivered against it in the past decade. The attitude of the Soviet Union will be of service to the movement, but the Union will not be responsible for it. The faith in an immediately impending world revolution has vanished in Asia as completely as in Europe. At first it seemed as if the suppressed nationalism of the colonial and quasi-colonial peoples, itself a product of Capitalism, and the grievances of the European national minorities, would provide the lever which could best set the revolutionary movement into operation against Imperialism. To-day the hope of this has been abandoned. Accordingly, Stalin now proposes to complete the Socialist development of the Soviet Union before any world revolution; for that the completed work in the Soviet Union is to provide the great incentive.

The example furnished by the solution of the problem of nationality in the Soviet Union is also to have a propaganda effect upon the peoples beyond its borders. Many of the peoples in the Soviet Union are related in race or language to neighbouring peoples across the frontier. The freedom and equality of rights accorded to the Ukrainians and White Russians in the Soviet Union are contrasted with the persecution and deprivation of rights to which they are exposed in Poland. The national freedom which the Koreans enjoy on the territory of the Soviet Union is contrasted with the oppression of Korea under the Japanese. Not a few of the autonomous national states that have come into existence along the borders of the Soviet Union owe their existence to the desire to apply the Leninist nationality policy in foreign affairs. Thus there was founded on the border of Bessarabia the Moldavian Republic, in which only about one-third of the inhabitants are Moldavians

—Roumanians as in Bessarabia, Roumania's annexation of which has not been recognized by the Soviet Union. Tiraspol, the capital of the new state, formerly an insignificant village, has become a centre of propaganda on the left bank of the Dniester. The case of the autonomous republic of Karelia is much the same; here again only about one-third of the population are Karelians, closely related to the neighbouring Finns. The eastern states of the Soviet Union in Central Asia and in Transcaucasia are ostentatious developments of the principle of equality of East and West within the Union; they are spearheads of Communist propaganda pointed eastwards. Baku, on a tongue of land in the Caspian, was intended at one time to be the centre of this propaganda; in one of the first years of the Communist regime a great congress of eastern peoples was held there. But since then the expectation of rapid and direct effects from propaganda in the East has dwindled away; the only two territories outside the Soviet Union in which the Soviet Government has gained effective influence, the Republic of Mongolia and the Republic of Tannu-Tuva, are former territories of the Chinese Empire which had already been virtually lost to it through the expansion of Tsarist Russia.[14]   The Mongols also are closely associated in religion, race, and language with peoples of the Soviet Union, the Buriats and the Kalmuks.

Whatever the effects abroad of the nationality policy of the Soviet Government, the main incentives to it were domestic.   There were three problems that called for solution: the constitutional one of the complete equality of rights of all nationalities and the abolition of all privileges of the Russian people, the social one of giving practical effect to the formal equality of rights by bringing the backward peoples up to the level of those that culturally and economically were the most advanced, and the intellectual one of introducing within the framework of the various national cultural systems the new universal Communist doctrine and faith.

NATIONALISM AND THE PROLETARIAT

Formally, though not intrinsically, the struggle of the proletariat against the bourgeoisie is in the first place a national one. The proletariat of each country must, naturally, begin by settling accounts with its own bourgeoisie.

The proletariat must begin with the conquest of political power, must raise itself to the position of the national class, must constitute itself the nation: in this sense it is itself national, though not at all in the sense of the bourgeoisie.

> MARX and ENGELS, in the *Communist Manifesto*.

The period of the dictatorship of the proletariat and of the building up of Socialism in the Soviet Union is the period of the flowering of the national civilizations, which while intrinsically Socialist are national in form.

> STALIN: Political report to the sixteenth congress of the Communist Party of the Soviet Union, July 1930.

UCCORDING to the census of 1926 the Soviet Anion is inhabited by 185 peoples, speaking 147 languages. Many of these populations are only parts of nations of which the greater part live beyond the borders of the Soviet Union, but some of them are represented in large numbers in the Union, for instance the Jews, the Germans, and the Poles; and all are being transformed in their national characteristics through the influence of Communism. Among them, as among the other peoples of the Soviet Union, the influence of the new spirit has been operative for too short a time to make much headway against the long-standing influences of their origin and of the traditions carried down through their language. But their young people are steadily absorbing the new ideas, and are beginning to strike out along entirely new paths, which are steadily carrying them away from their racial kindred beyond the frontier and assimilating them to the youth of the other Soviet peoples. Among these populations the intellectual transformation is of more importance than the political problem, and it is so also among the many small ethnical groups, each of no more than a few thousand souls, which are to be found especially in Siberia and in the northern Caucasus. These small groups are in many cases at an extremely low cultural level, and seemed in the past to be destined ultimately to die out; the Soviet Government has devoted particular attention to them in its nationality policy.

But amid all the variety of the national composition of the Soviet Union, there are only a few national groups that are of numerical importance. Five groups account together for more than 84 per cent of the population of the Union, no other group reaching as much as 2 per cent of the total population. The principal group is that of the Russians, who are no longer a minority, as in the old Russian Empire, but form 53 per cent of the population. Next come the Ukrainians, with some 21 per cent, and then, at a long distance after them, the White Russians, the third Slav people of the Union; the Kazaks, formerly known as Kirghiz, inhabiting the wide steppes between western Siberia, central Asia, and the southern Volga; and the Uzbeks in central Asia. Eight more national groups embrace over a million souls apiece—the Tartars of the Volga and the Crimea, the Jews, the Georgians, the Turks of Azerbaijan, the Armenians in Transcaucasia, the Mordvins or Volga Finns, the Germans, and the Tchuvash of the Nizhni Novgorod area.

But many of the peoples that count less than a million souls present political problems through the development of their national consciousness and through their geographical situation—as, for instance, the 764,000 nomad Turcomans of central Asia or the 238,000 Buriats of eastern Siberia. The Buriats tried in the years following the world war to set up an independent Buriat–Mongol State which should revive the old glories of the Mongols, who formerly dominated vast areas.

The peoples of the Soviet Union fall into four main groups, entirely separate in origin and language. The first to come into contact in the course of their history with the three branches of the Slav language-group, the Russians, Ukrainians, and White Russians, were the Finnish–Ugrian races, inhabiting the unending forests and marshes of central and north-eastern Russia. These Finnish peoples, the Komi, the Mari, and the Mordvins, were steadily pushed back by the Russians into less fruitful areas with severe climates, and were deprived by the Russian Government of every sort of provision for cultural or social welfare; they remained poor peasant populations, at the lowest level of culture, and only began to develop a literature after the Revolution. On a considerably higher plane were certain branches of the Turco-Tartar ethnical group, which is spread over the whole of the vast area that stretches eastwards from the Volga and the Black Sea to the Pacific. To this group belong the Tartars of the Volga and the Crimea, who already had before the world war an urban bourgeoisie, a nationalist movement, and a secular literature; the Tchuvash, who had been converted to the Orthodox faith and brought within the realm of Russian culture before the Revolution; the impoverished peasant people of the Bashkirs in the western Urals, who had also suffered the loss of all their good and fruitful lands under the ruthless colonization policy of the Russian Government; and the nomad and semi-nomad Kazaks and Kirghiz (the latter were formerly called Karakirghiz or Mountain Kirghiz in distinction from the Kazaks, who were known as Kirghiz). The Uzbeks of central Asia, the dominant race in the former Emirate of Bokhara, had a developed civilization of an eastern feudal type. Ready supporters of the idea of pan-Islamism were to be found among the Uzbek aristocracy and priesthood. More primitive were their western neighbours and stubborn enemies, the nomad Turcomans, who inhabit the desert and the oases between the Amu-Daria and the Caspian Sea. On the other shore of the Caspian, in the southern Caucasus, the Turco-Tartar race is represented by the Turks of Azerbaijan (they are called Turks by the Russians) who showed themselves amenable to modernist influences, to the adoption of the Latin alphabet and to women's emancipation, earlier than the other races to whom they are akin. In the Far East, Turco-Tartars are represented by the Yakuts, who have adopted the Greek Orthodox religion; they inhabit a vast region with great potentialities, stretching from Lake Baikal to the northern Pacific. Amid the mixture of populations of the northern Caucasus, where isolated valleys, difficult of access, have favoured the survival of small and even diminutive ethnical groups, and the continuance of their particular characteristics and language, there are not only Turco-Tartar but Caucasian peoples; their principal representatives, Georgians and Armenians, peoples with an ancient, highly developed culture, a wide measure of social differentiation, and advanced national movements, inhabit the southern slopes of the Caucasus. It has already been mentioned that the Soviet Union contains, in addition to primitive Siberian peoples, Mongol races of Buddhist religion.

This multiplicity of national types, of which only the most general indication has been given here, is but one of the obstacles, and not the most serious, to the solution of the nationality problem of the Soviet Union. The proclamation had been made of the full equality of rights between the various peoples, and this principle was strictly adhered to. No pride of race is tolerated, even in relation to eastern and primitive peoples; the slightest suggestion of any predominance of the Russian race or of any tendency towards Russification is carefully avoided. The old name of the Russian Empire has been replaced by the supra-national name Union of Soviet Socialist Republics. All the more important peoples of the Union inhabiting definite territories have been endowed with territorial autonomy adjusted to their importance, their degree of development, and the extent of the territory they inhabit. The principal territories are member states of the Union, described in the constitutional literature of the Union as sovereign

F

states which entered voluntarily into the Union, ceding to it a part of their sovereign rights but retaining under the Constitution the indefeasible right of secession. Other territories form Autonomous Socialist Soviet Republics, or Autonomous Regions, within the member states; these two types are not to be described as states but as administrative units delimited according to the national composition of the population. The original member states of the Union were the Russian Socialist Federative Soviet Republic, the Ukraine, White Russia, and Transcaucasia. The R.S.F.S.R. embraces eleven autonomous republics and fifteen autonomous regions, but in spite of its name it must be regarded not as a federation of several states but as a single state with extensive decentralization. Transcaucasia, on the other hand, is a true federal state. Its three member states, Armenia, Azerbaijan, and Georgia, which had declared their independence after the collapse of Tsarism, fought bitterly against one another for some years, until their transformation into soviet states was effected; subsequently national peace was secured in the Caucasus, and the Transcaucasian Socialist Federal Soviet Republic was formed, on December 12, 1922.

On December 30 in the same year the Union of Soviet Socialist Republics (U.S.S.R.) was established.

At first the Soviet Union was mainly composed of western Slav states; this was no longer the case after 1925, when the central Asian soviet states of Uzbekistan and Turkmenistan were admitted into the Union. After the fall of Tsarism Bokhara and Khiva, formerly Russian vassal states, had been proclaimed People's Soviet Republics, as was Mongolia later; the Russian "general government"* of Turkestan was attached as an autonomous republic to the R.S.F.S.R. These territorial divisions were the outcome of events in the nineteenth century; their frontiers had been determined by the absorption of khanates in the course of Russia's career of conquest, and had no relation to the national composition of the populations. In 1924 central Asia was divided up afresh on ethnical lines, and there came into existence the two Soviet Republics of Uzbekistan and Turkmenistan, which became member states of the Soviet Union in May 1925. The republic of Tadjikistan, inhabited by the Tadjiks, who are

* That is, province administered by a Governor-General.

Shiite Moslems, was partitioned off from Uzbekistan, becoming in 1929 the seventh member state of the Soviet Union, in which the eastern federal states are now in a majority.

The Soviet Union is a national complex consisting of 42 autonomous units constitutionally interwoven in a multiplicity of ways. Nine of these are federal member states, 15 autonomous republics, and 18 autonomous regions. The supreme power in the state is the All-union Soviet Congress, which assembles in alternate years and elects the All-union Central Executive Committee; this consists of two Chambers—the Federal Council, with a membership proportioned to the population of the various member states, and the Nationalities' Council, to which the various member states and autonomous republics send five representatives each and the autonomous regions one each. The Presidium of the Central Executive Committee has seven chairmen, one for each member state. The conduct of foreign policy, defence, and transport is vested in the Union; economic, financial, and labour questions come within the joint competence of the Union and the member states; law, public health, welfare organization and education are reserved to the member states and the autonomous republics and regions.

In this way all the more important of the peoples of the Soviet Union have been accorded self-government. But this territorial solution did not suffice in all cases. Some peoples, above all the Jews, did not inhabit any definitely delimited area; others count only a few thousand souls and are thus not in a position to carry on a separate state existence of their own. And the nationalities in the Soviet Union have largely spread into one another's areas, so that there are many national groups living outside the territory of their nationality—Russians in the Ukraine, Ukrainians in Russia, Germans (apart from the German Volga Republic)[15] in the Ukraine and the Crimea, Tartars in Bashkir territory, Uzbeks in Tadji-kistan—so that there is scarcely a people in the Soviet Union which has not members who form a minority in one or very often in many member states or regions. The Soviet Union has accordingly enacted very elaborate minority legislation, assuring to the minorities their schools and the official employment of their mother tongue; wherever minorities live together in villages or districts, they have been brought together in administrative units in which their language and their national characteristics have full play.

But this formal equality could not suffice for Communism; it was bound to work for an economic and cultural uplifting of the backward populations to the level of the most advanced, the Russian. In this work the energies of the Revolution were directed along two channels. The Russian people had itself to be transformed in all the cultural and economic elements of its existence; and the Soviet Government had to set to work with redoubled energy and to effect a much more radical "westernization" among the backward peoples. The tasks which the Communist Party has set itself on the social plane, the industrialization of the country-side, the creation of a rural proletariat, the cultural uplifting of the masses and a comprehensive system of popular education, become thus the first condition for the solution of the nationalities problem. The building up of Socialism and the nationalities policy have to be carried on in conjunction with one another by the proletariat and its "vanguard," the Communist Party. The trouble was that among most of the non-Russian peoples there was neither the one nor the other—neither a proletariat nor Communists. Consequently, though the new solution of the nationality problem was a great advance on its predecessor, it had still, as in Tsarist times, to be presented to the outlying populations from the centre of the Russian realm, had to be imposed on them, and was Moscow's policy and not theirs. It had similarly to be imposed on the Russian people, but with the other peoples there was the added difficulty of the memories of past oppression from Moscow. If the new policy was not to be wrecked in advance on the mistrust of populations that had learnt in the course of decades or centuries that only evil could come to them from Moscow and from the Russians, it had to be applied with careful regard to the national feelings of these populations. Its greatest danger was, therefore, the "Pan-Russian chauvinism" (as it is called in the official Communist terminology), dating from the immediate past and not yet by any means forgotten—the old tendency that had regarded itself as the pillar of Russian imperial loyalties and had stood determinedly for the maintenance of the privileged position of the Russian element and culture within the empire. This spirit continued to show itself in the ranks of the Party and the proletariat, and in their representatives who had to carry out the new policy in the outlying areas

of the Union among the non-Russian populations.

The Communist Party recognized the right
of peoples to self-determination, but it demanded
for the working class and for the Party a unified
organization over and above all differences of
nationality. Even before the world war it had
resolutely opposed every attempt to differentiate
between the Socialist parties of differing nationality in a country or the various national groups of
workmen in a village or a factory, or to organize
them separately according to nationality. The
unity of the working class as supporter of a
unified policy, and the unity of the Party repre-
senting this policy, were, in the Party's view,
indispensable conditions of a proletarian policy.
As all peoples were to be brought within the field
of this policy, a working class had to be created
and cells of the Communist Party established
among all peoples. Many peoples, however, in
the Soviet Union had few town workers or
Socialists or Party members, or none at all.[16]
The interior of Russia was mainly a country of
peasants, and the distant territories still more so.
The urban population of the Soviet Union was
some 19 per cent of the whole; the proportion in

the Tartar Republic was 11 per cent, in Kazakistan 8 per cent, and in the republics of the
Tchuvash and the Yakuts only some 5 per cent—
and of the urban population in these and other
outlying territories the bulk were Russians or
others of external origin. Of every 10,000
occupied persons in the Soviet Union only 338
were engaged in industry, but in most of the outlying territories the figure ranged between 85
and 9, and here again the percentage of indigenous workers was considerably smaller than
that of Russians. In Turkmenistan the Russian
workers accounted for more than a quarter of the
Russian population, scarcely 2 per cent of the
Turcomans being industrial workers. Even in
the most advanced national areas, such as the
Ukraine, the proportion between town and
country was not very different. The town
workers were mainly Russians, the Ukrainians
were almost exclusively peasants. As recently
as 1923 the membership of the Communist
Party of the Ukraine was 52 per cent Russian
and only 23 per cent Ukrainian. In 1924 the
party organization in Kazakistan counted only
5 per cent of Kazaks. Thus, during the earliest
years after the Revolution the state, trade union,

and party machinery were of necessity entirely or predominantly in Russian hands.

The only remedy for this unsatisfactory situation lay in the social, cultural, and economic transformation of the masses among the non-Russian populations. Thus the improvement of their conditions of existence and their standard of education, the introduction of industries and a co-operative system, the building of schools and the campaign against illiteracy, all served a double purpose. They aimed not only at giving practical shape to the theoretical equality between the various peoples, but also at preparing the way for the progressive staffing of the state, trade union, and party services in the outlying territories with members of the indigenous population, thus making it a full partner in social and state affairs. Nuclei of indigenous proletarians and Communists had to be trained if there was to be such a thing as self-government among the non-Russian populations of the Soviet Union. The government and party machinery had to be "rooted," to use the official term, in the indigenous population, as the Soviet state could only so be assured of the active co-operation of the broad masses among all its peoples.. In recent years the Soviet Government and the Party have bent their energies particularly to this task of raising the cultural level of the various peoples of the Union to a common standard. For all the success that they have had in this field, the Soviet authorities make no secret of the fact that this goal is very far from having yet been attained, and that many years' work lies still ahead of them in radically transforming the conditions of existence among the backward peoples.

The proletarian state and the Socialist economic order are borne on the shoulders of the proletariat. Universal education and the introduction of modern technical progress have as their purpose the training of proletarians equal to the task of building up the Socialist state. In the process of the industrialization of the Soviet Union, the outlying territories have made a greater percentage of industrial advance over their pre-revolutionary state than has the interior of Russia. The Tsarist centralization of industry, with the outlying territories treated virtually as colonies within the empire, has been abandoned in favour of a deliberate decentralization. This was at the same time more in the interest of the whole Eurasian realm, and the shifting eastwards of the centre of industrial activity has bound the vast country in a closer unity. Great industrial enterprises have sprung up in the outlying areas of the Union. New transport routes, such as the line connecting Siberia with Turkestan,[17] have opened up territories hitherto inaccessible to modern trade and industry, and their construction and working have drawn the indigenous population into the ranks of the workers. All this has no such purpose as the creation of economic self-sufficiency in the various territories or any promotion of economic nationalism; that would not only be in conflict with the needs and the principles of Socialist construction, but would make impossible any economic progress.

The new economic system aims at embracing not only the towns and industry but agriculture. The electrification planned for the whole of the Union, with its influence on country life, has already been carried far in Transcaucasia, with its mountain streams. The aim is to increase the equipment and the credit provision for the indigenous peasants to the level of the Russians, which, low as it was, was far above that of the "Inorodtzi." The mechanization of the countryside, the setting up of kolkhozi and sovkhozi, or collective and state farms, has proceeded in many cases farther in the outlying territories than in the centre. Armenia, which possessed not a single tractor in 1914, now has over 600. In Kazakistan and other territories the settlement of the nomad tribes, who lost their means of existence through the perishing of their herds during the famine years, has been energetically pursued. Being settled in collective farms, they are passing at a single step to a socialized and mechanized farming.

This economic and social transformation means a conflict with mediæval traditions and customs. The Soviet Government has had to enter on this in the eastern territories with more caution and circumspection than in the interior of Russia. Among the Mohammedan peoples, with whom religion and tradition have shown more vitality than among the Slavs, the Government has met with fierce resistance. A characteristic case is that of the efforts to secure women's emancipation. Among the Mohammedans of central Asia women were only permitted to leave home heavily veiled and completely unrecognizable. The purchase of wives and carrying off of women were still general customs; schools for girls were non-existent. Here juridical and economic equality for women meant a revolutionizing of the whole of social life. In its earliest years the Soviet Government had to make many concessions in central Asia; the old customs were left untouched, the Koran continued to be taught in many schools, and the Mohammedan ecclesiastical courts continued to administer jurisdiction at a time when all this had long gone by the board in European Russia. Not until 1927 did the propaganda for the emancipation of the "women workers of the East" set in in full force. Special committees were set up for the purpose in Moscow and in the various territories concerned; wife-purchase and rapine were declared punishable offences, though the Soviet Government, unlike modern Turkey, continued to avoid any direct measures of compulsion against the veil. To-day in such advanced Mohammedan territories as the Crimea the veil has completely disappeared. Tartar girls are increasingly attending the state schools and are rapidly adopting the Communist ways of life of European Russia; on the Corso in Simferopol they are hardly distinguishable in appearance and manner from Russian girls; they have already become members of the Communist youth organizations.

In central Asia the veil is still to be found. Many Mohammedan women acclaimed the emancipation movement with great enthusiasm, welcomed the new world that opened before them, and were far ahead of the men in eagerness to learn and desire for progress. All the more stubborn was in many cases the opposition of the men to the emancipation of the women. In many cases the women had to pay with their lives for laying aside the veil or for other modernizing tendencies; a husband or a father or brothers became the avengers of family honour and tradition. At first it was out of the question to bring women and men into common schools and clubs, and in towns and villages and encampments in the East special schools and reading-rooms and clubs were established for women. "Red Yurts" and "Red Kibitkas" were instituted in the areas inhabited by nomads and semi-nomads —transportable tents with which teacher and doctor and midwife and library went from camp to camp, held courses of instruction in reading and writing, in hygiene and the care of children, made the women acquainted with their rights, and tried to organize them. The "mountain women's huts" worked in a similar way in the

Caucasian mountains and their remote and isolated valleys. The committees for the improvement of the conditions of women's life and work have begun to organize the home-workers in co-operatives. One of the purposes of the industrialization now beginning in these regions and the setting up of the kolkhozi is to bring the masses of the women out of their seclusion, liberate them from their absorption in domestic duties, and engage them in production. In the eastern soviet states 1500 women have been elected chairmen of village soviets in recent years. Eighteen women hold leading positions in Uzbekistan; one is deputy chairman of the Central Executive Committee of the Republic. The Supreme Court of Justice in Kazakistan has a woman president; another woman is a member of the Council of People's Commissars.

This beginning of women's emancipation is radically changing the conditions of existence among the eastern peoples. Like every other campaign of liberation, it has had its martyrs. The young woman who ventured to break through the bonds of tradition had in the first years, in spite of the protection of the soviet authorities, to endure a veritable martyrdom. In remote parts of the country many Mohammedan ecclesiastical courts took action before the soviet authorities could intervene, condemning "unfaithful" women and those who left their marital homes in order to begin a new life, to death by stoning. Not until the Communist Party had gained strength among the indigenous elements did it become possible to take energetic steps to combat the influence of the Mohammedan priesthood and the feudal landowners and to fight against the old social "prejudices," in which the religion was included. To-day the struggle against Islam and its habits of life, against the mosque and the mullahs, is being carried on with the same energy as against the church or the synagogue.

This propaganda lies largely in the hands of indigenous elements. Had it been merely imposed from without, from Moscow, it would have called forth the strongest opposition from the whole people and would have strengthened nationalist influences. To-day the Communist movement is steadily advancing among the youth of the Mohammedan peoples, young men and women alike, and with the support of this active group soviet propaganda is able to preach the new way of living among the eastern peoples.

G

In the more advanced Mohammedan countries, in Tartary, Azerbaijan, and the Crimea,
the propaganda has already met with great
success. It had the support of the progressive
intellectuals in these countries, who even before
the world war had been advocates of far-reaching
secularization of culture and of public life, and
after the war had held up the example of Turkey's
radical westernization. Azerbaijan was the
first Mohammedan state to replace the Arabic
alphabet—even before Kemalist Turkey did—
with the Latin alphabet, and to adopt legislation
for women's emancipation. Baku, the capital of
Azerbaijan, is the seat of a great petroleum
industry of the most modern type, and has thus
been a pioneer in modernization.

A clear picture of the transformation of Islam
in the Soviet Union is offered by the Crimea.
Bakhtchisserai, the old and historic capital of the
Khanate of Crimea, lies some thirty kilometres
south of Simferopol, picturesquely grouped
around a few slender Turkish minarets on the
slopes of the Crimean foothills. It is inhabited
entirely by Tartars. Until recent years it was a
centre of Mohammedan piety and ancient undisturbed traditions. The advanced intellectuals

among the Tartars, advocates of reforms and of a modern type of nationalism, saw in Bakhtchisserai a hotbed of reaction. Here, as in many other places in the former Tsarist empire, the Revolution was followed by the declaration of a national bourgeois republic. After the conquest of the Crimea by the Soviet Government, the Communist Party found an entire absence of Tartar proletarian elements or Communists in the Crimea, and had in the early years to rely on the support of the advanced nationalist intellectuals. For years the administration of the Autonomous Socialist Soviet Republic of Crimea lay in the hands of bourgeois nationalist Tartars, who set their hopes, under the banner of Communism, on the rebirth of the old khanate, the memories of which probably greatly exaggerated its old splendour. To-day that is all in the past. Years of work among the Tartars have strengthened the Communist movement sufficiently to enable the administration of the country to be placed in hands which steer strictly along the course desired by Moscow.

Bakhtchisserai itself has undergone a complete change, typical of the course of development. The Arabic signs have almost entirely disappeared, and remain only in a few corners on the signboards of an old firm here and there. The streets of the town, with their names in Latin letters, are reminiscent of Turkey. Only a few years ago Bakhtchisserai was the centre of orthodox Islam in the Crimea. The little town then had thirty-three mosques; to-day only three are used. The number of the Faithful has rapidly shrunk; the youth have turned their backs on the mosque. Everywhere there are still signs of the past, but the little town, once so busy, has been hit hard by the transformation of the whole economic system. The old eastern leisureliness is still there, but the old security and easy-going cheerfulness are gone. Life here is doubly melancholy and oppressive, away from the great centres of industrialization and almost untouched by the strong pulsations of the new life with its vigorous forward urge. When Islam flourished the town had importance; now it is a diminutive moribund village, battered by the winds of a new age but still unadjusted to it.

The old palace of the khan is open to the public, and has been turned into a museum of the type of those which have been set up in recent years in all the new national republics and territories.

Its exhibits show the popular arts and customs of the Tartars, their handicrafts and farming methods, their history and civilization. Here the nation's past is to be preserved for a new age that has dawned over the country. Alongside it have been exhibited the present and the future, and effective propagandist diagrams show the economic and cultural progress of the Crimea during the years of soviet rule, the setting of the Tartars on a footing of equality, and the educative work performed among them.

Such old Tartar towns as Bakhtchisserai stand alien and untouched alongside the new typical towns of the Russian colonizers, such as Simferopol. In other towns, such as Yalta, a mutual adjustment steadily proceeds between the two elements. The difference between the colonizing people and the subject people is disappearing. The equalization of rights of all nationalities and the Europeanization and westernization of the whole Eurasian federation are beginning to bring the various peoples of the Soviet Union closer to one another, to standardize their way of living, and to train them to be the bearers of a new and common culture.[18]

LANGUAGE AND CULTURE

The period of the dictatorship of the proletariat and of the building up of Socialism in the Soviet Union is the period of the flowering of the national civilizations, which while intrinsically Socialist are national in form.

> STALIN: Political report to the sixteenth congress of the Communist . Party of the Soviet Union, July 1930.

The national divisions and oppositions between the peoples are disappearing more and more with the development of the bourgeoisie, with freedom of trade, the world market, and the uniformity of industrial production and of the conditions of living which it involves.

The rule of the proletariat will make them disappear yet more. In proportion as the exploitation of one individual by another is brought to an end, the exploitation of one nation by another will be ended.

With the falling away of the opposition between classes in the nation there falls away the hostile attitude between nations.

> MARX and ENGELS, in the *Communist Manifesto*.

The Soviet Union is in theory a supra-national state. It knows no nation as the wielder of the authority of the state; it is not the organized form of the will of a nation, like the European states since the French Revolution. The Soviet state rests on the class of the proletariat; the state serves the will of the proletariat to persist and progress; it is becoming the expression and the protector of the creative efforts of the proletariat. Hence the Soviet Union is free from every attempt at cultural or lingual oppression or subordination of the smaller peoples or minorities in its territory. A definite common body of culture is being bestowed on the masses, but not through the Russian language but through the languages of the various peoples; and the culture is not a national, a Russian culture but a supra-national, proletarian, Communist one. Similarly European missions in the East did not always propagate the culture of any European nationality, but often a supra-national one, unfamiliar to the eastern peoples, that of the European and American bourgeois world, Protestant or Catholic. They did this, however, through the medium of languages which were not those of the people; and they did not try as a rule to promote and influence the indigenous literature, but put in its place a language strange and unfamiliar to the young people of the country. Thus they inevitably tore the "educated youth" from their natural environment, severed the bond between them and the masses, and left the masses in their old life, without economic or cultural assistance.

The cultural propaganda of Communism, on the contrary, is carried on in the languages of the indigenous peoples. This was only possible after comprehensive preparatory work. For many peoples a literature of their own had to be created, or their existing literature enriched and perfected. Under the Soviet Government there came into existence scientific associations for research into the national culture of the indigenous populations and their past history; libraries and museums were founded, and the national traditions of the masses in artistic expression, in theatre, dance, and music, were cultivated. The aim was to produce a culture national in form, above all in language, but supra-national, Socialist, or proletarian, in essence. The national form was approved not for the sake of its intrinsic value but as the medium of a new culture embracing all humanity. As in the past Christianity and Islam, and later Capitalism had wrested the national cultures from their isolation, had approximated them to one another and subjected them to new general standards, so Communism proposes now to do in yet more effective ways.

But the promotion of the national cultures, the research into their past, brought to life again many historic memories; the cultivation of popular traditions in art and literature strongly reinforced the love of all that was characteristically national, and of the national language, now flourishing once more (or even, in many cases, for the first time) and inspired with new life. It aroused also the ambition in each people to promote the national culture and its content, product of the traditions of the past, with all the individualization of its character in its inherited and now conscious racial vitality. The people began to be aware of its own value, to believe in its historic mission, to see its past in a romantic transfiguration and to love it. It might easily happen that the revivified past would be set against the new present, a present concerned only for the future, and aiming at producing for all men a peaceful and creative life together, based on a rational view of social realities, and taming

the irrational forces of selfish group-egotism that
have come down from the darkness of the past.
Thus, by a paradoxical process, the cultural
nationality policy of the Soviet Government was
in danger of awakening or reinforcing the
nationalism and the nationalistic ambitions of the
peoples of the Union. Yet it was impossible for
the peoples to be prepared for the acceptance
of the new Socialist culture, the proletarian
religion of science and technique, except through
the awakening of cultural activities, the association
of the broad masses with them, and their intellectual ripening, together with the raising of the
economic and general standard of living. The
Soviet Government placed its trust in the training
of the youth, in the alertness and adaptability
of its policy, and in the changing economic and
social conditions, for success in pushing on,
past the awakened or accentuated cultural
nationalism of the peoples, to the desired intrinsically uniform human culture which would only
vary from people to people in form, in the
language medium. The lingual and cultural
autonomy of the peoples of the Soviet Union
was to produce out of the slogan of the right of
national self-determination a solution of the

nationality problem in accordance with the principles of Communism.

Before the development of political nationalism in modern times, speech was simply the natural means of expression, not an instrument of policy. The people spoke a dialect that bound them not with the state and its political pursuit of power but with the home and the village; the state and science employed a supra-national language scarcely spoken by any people. It is modern nationalism that raised the popular speech to the language of literature and the state. Fichte made the intimate connexion between nationality and language the starting-point of his theory of nationalism. In the state of the nineteenth century, which had become what it had never been before, the highest form of organization of the nation, which identified itself with this state, the national language became a constitutional function, the means of the will of the nation to dominance. Where the state embraced several peoples, there now developed an oppression, unknown until then, of the other peoples by the nation that identified itself with the state; this nation's dominance in the state found expression in the position given to its language. The laws concerning the use of the official language in Czechoslovakia or Poland, which figure so prominently in the constitutional law of these countries, depress the minority peoples, through the subordinate position given to their languages, to citizens of an inferior class, deprive them of many otherwise natural rights, and hit them in the most sensitive place. The struggle for the privileged position of the official language in administration and justice, in school and parliament, is the favourite scene of the orgies of nationalism. It is over this question that the national zeal of the minority populations flares up, that the struggle for the rights and the prestige of peoples is waged, that the natural element of the language of the people is turned into a hotly contested political instrument. In pre-revolutionary Russia the Russian language was the one and only official language and the principal means employed in the attempt to denationalize the non-Russian populations. The proletarian state, no longer the expression of the will to dominance of a nation, no longer recognizes an official language, the constitutionally established privilege of a particular language. In the Soviet Union there is no talk of an official language but only of languages in general use, all of which have equal rights. Every population has the right to use its own language in government offices and courts of justice, in soviet and school. All proclamations and notices are framed in the language of the region or district. Language thus ceases to be a subject of policy or a question of power. It loses nothing in this way in cultural value, but a good deal politically in emotional appeal. Now that the Russian language is no longer privileged or imposed, it is developing by free consent into a lingua franca for the multi-lingual Union.

The populations of the Soviet Union not only enjoy the right to use their own mother tongue; the Government has from the first done everything to promote the development of these popular tongues, hampered as it had been by the authority of the Tsarist state, to encourage their literature, and to educate the masses of the people in their language and literature. In view of the heritage which the Revolution took over from Tsarist times, that had to be done at the expense of the Russian language and its past privileged position. With few exceptions, such as Georgian and Armenian, the popular tongues of the Tsarist empire had developed no literature worth mention.

Many possessed neither a literary heritage nor even an alphabet. The masses were unable to read or write; there were no schools in which their mother tongue was used. The upper classes among many peoples, for instance the Ukrainians and the White Russians, had been completely assimilated to Russian or Polish culture. Thus the Soviet Government had to build afresh from the foundations in the field of national culture. But this very fact, that in many cases it had to deal with new social strata innocent of the rudiments of culture, with no educational tradition, no modern literature accessible to the masses, lightened the task of the soviets in giving to the newly created or revivified national literatures an entirely new cultural content. The Government was thus able to register many successes in a short time in this field.

The general principles of Soviet cultural policy —the combating of illiteracy, the introduction of compulsory education, the spread of socialistic and popular scientific literature among the masses, the bringing of women into public life—necessarily, since everything was done in the mother tongue, contributed to the development of the national languages and literatures.[19]   The task was tremendous. Teachers had to be trained from the midst of every population, school books provided,[20] and for a number of languages alphabets had to be elaborated. Many of the eastern peoples have a religious literature, but their languages were inadequate to the needs of modern life and science. Among many peoples it is still impossible to lecture in the colleges in the mother tongue in any but the literary faculty; technical faculties are compelled to use Russian. By the end of 1933, however, there are to be sufficient teachers and sufficient lingual preparation to enable all faculties to use the language of the peoples.

The same attention has been devoted to educational work among adults. In the capitals of the national republics and territories scholars and academies provide for the issue of dictionaries, publishing institutions and libraries for the spread of books, theatres and museums, historical and other scientific societies for the various aspects of national culture. Film and wireless play their part in the service of the building up of this culture. Government officials and the members of the different economic bodies are required to learn the language of the local population, and are steadily being replaced by members of the indigenous population as these are trained to competence. This process is still far from completion. It is going on simultaneously with the general training of the peoples in Communism.

The new alphabets were compiled not on the basis of the Russian but of the Latin alphabet. The Turco-Tartar peoples, who had used the Arabic alphabet, have gone over to the Latin one. As in many other measures of "westernization," the Turkish Republic has taken the same step. Reactionary nationalist groups in the Soviet Union, and the Mohammedan priesthood, offered opposition to the reform of the alphabet, but in accordance with resolutions of the first Turcological congress in Baku in 1926 and of the congress of the All-Union Committee on the new Latin alphabet in June 1927, the Latin script was introduced in place of Arabic throughout the Union on August 7, 1929. As the masses among the eastern poples were unable to read or write, and in many eastern tongues there was no secular literature of any moment, it was possible to introduce the new alphabet simultaneously with the campaign against illiteracy.

The Mongol and Iranian and some of the Caucasian languages of the Soviet Union were also converted to the Latin alphabet, the old literary languages, where they existed, assimilated to the popular speech, and divested of their associations with the classic religious literature and the mediæval past of the peoples. In this way humanistic languages accessible only to a small educated circle, and that usually means theologically educated, were turned into popular literary languages aimed at meeting the needs of the new life with its resources in modern technique and science.

These are processes familiar to all peoples that have awakened to modern national consciousness and have thus entered the era of secularization. Under the guidance of the Communist Party the process of raising the popular tongues to literary languages followed the lines of the new proletarian culture. Simplicity and popularization were aimed at everywhere.[21] The conference of German teachers in the Soviet Union which assembled in June 1931 in Pokrovsk, the capital of the autonomous German Volga Republic, recommended the simplification of German spelling with the aim of "the provision of a

H

proletarian German language which shall be intelligible to all, clear, concise, and natural." Gothic script should no longer be used in teaching. In a resolution dealing with general principles the Pokrovsk Conference protested against the practice of certain German soviet teachers in allowing themselves to be guided by the example of Germany: Germany could not serve as an example for the Germans in the Soviet Union in the field of cultural constructive work. Only the republic's own Communist school books should be used, not books imported from Germany. This standpoint is characteristic of the cultural nationality policy of the Soviet Union. It means the separation from large national bodies such as the Germans and the Jews of the sections of those groups living in the Soviet Union. The policy aims at creating a Communist Jewish people within the Soviet Union, a Communist German people, with no cultural association with that which in the course of centuries of development has become German or Jewish culture, and has hitherto been the basis of the intellectual life of the Jews and Germans living in the Soviet Union. This applies not only to those peoples of whom only a minority lives within the Soviet Union, but also to all others, especially those who can look back on an old historic culture. The cultural nationality policy of the Communist Party signifies, amid all the educational work on behalf of the masses, "death to the national culture," at all events to the national culture that has developed in the course of centuries and flourished in the age of bourgeois nationalism. In place of it there is to come a new common Socialist culture, with a way of living determined by new and rising sociological strata of the population, who have been scarcely touched by the old culture. This new way of living is being proclaimed and set up in every field, and finds its representatives and pioneers in the Soviet youth of all the peoples in the vast Soviet Union.

The Communist state can grant entire lingual autonomy and liberty, but it cannot recognize cultural autonomy and liberty. The doctrinal content of Marxism must be given expression in every tongue, as it has to be carried to every people. The state sets out accordingly to develop and assist every tongue; all are equal in its view, as in its view all men, whatever their endowment, are equal. It cannot, however, recognize the elements of national culture that belong to the feudal and theocratic epoch or the bourgeois capitalist epoch, and have established themselves in philosophy, poetry, and art, and often in habits of life. The characteristic and distinguishing elements in existing national cultures, their specific values anchored in the past and drawn, in the course of the life of generations, from the inspiration of a particular territory and a history that cannot repeat itself, values represented always by the upper classes, remain alien to it. Its purpose is to set the cultural life of all peoples on a new basis. Accordingly it destroys the bonds that unite the life of the people with the past. That means death to the national cultures, especially among peoples with a culture that is particularly strongly rooted in history and gives vivid expression to the consciousness of that history, a culture that is not merely the possession of a small class but has inspired the whole life of the people with its intellectual content, has intellectually formed the people. The Soviet Government has no desire at all for the assimilation or the extinction of the Jewish people, it envisages in the future a Jewish, Yiddish-speaking people as vigorous and as thoroughly imbued with the Communist idea as Russians or Tartars or Buriats. But the Jewish people of the Union must be entirely dissociated from Judaism; instruction in the Hebrew language and the perpetuation of Jewish religious culture as it has been developed through more than three thousand years, forming and giving outward expression to the characteristic spirit of the Jewish people, are forbidden. The Jewish people is thus cut off entirely from the sources of its culture. The same experience has fallen to the lot of the Mohammedan peoples of the Soviet Union, whose culture rested on Islam, on the Koran, and on the knowledge of the Arabic language and culture. Only the popular elements of the existing national cultures, unassociated with traditional religion and close to the life of the masses, are to be retained and interwoven with the new uniform Socialist culture, the attainment of which is the purpose of all education in the Soviet Union. In the new state, culture and art are enrolled in the service of the creation of the new Socialist order, and with them the national cultures, which are to be national in form but proletarian in content.

The youth of all the Soviet peoples are trained to a sense of class solidarity and to a realization of the interdependence of all peoples, and in all the various tongues, the use of which is entirely free, the same doctrine is taught, the same song intoned. The very fact that the Soviet Government is endowing many peoples of the Union and the broad masses of nearly every people for the first time with a generous measure of cultural benefits and education, makes it possible to attempt to fill the national cultures with a new and uniform content. And just as this uniformity of the Communist faith is pervading all cultural life, and so creating unity and association amid all the chartered variety of the national tongues, so the unity of the Communist Party is throwing a powerful bond and an iron fetter around the multiplicity of the autonomous national territorial formations of which, in accordance with the principle of national self-determination, the Union of Soviet Socialist Republics is composed.

A Soviet professor of constitutional law, Professor Gurvitch, has stated in his commentary on the Constitution of the Soviet Union that under it "every people possesses the political and juridical form of existence which best corresponds to its powers and its opportunities of development. All peoples are equal in rights and in consideration as children of the Soviet family, which effectually realizes the great slogan, 'Proletarians of all countries, unite!' " This formula of Professor Gurvitch's is right in its statement that all peoples of the Soviet Union are entirely equal in rights and in consideration. But free in their political form and in their development they are not. They are free only within the narrow limits permitted by a Socialist Soviet Republic. Their very Constitutions are almost identical in wording. But even the Constitutions, with their direct and democratic participation of the masses in the conduct of the business of the state, are not a reality but a programme, a goal which the ruling party has set for the training of the masses.

Of late the tendency has grown continually stronger, and more openly admitted, to regard the machinery of the Soviet state as a mere executive organ of the general policy of the Party. Amid all the autonomy and "independence" given to the national republics and territories, there remains always the unity of the Communist Party as a supra-national organization. And it is the Party that really makes the decision in every question, not the organs of the various national republics. One of Stalin's closest collaborators, Kaganovitch, in his report on the results of the plenary session of the central committee of the Party in December 1930, emphasizes that the soviets, the state machinery, are lagging behind the tempo of the general policy of the Party, but that the actual unity of action between the organs of Party and state must be assured——that is, that the leadership in the soviets from the highest posts in the Union and the various republics down to the villages must be thoroughly imbued with the general policy of the Party. The peoples of the Soviet Union enjoy full equality of rights, but it is an equality before the law, equal and uniform for them all, of the Communist Party, whose instructions are carried out through the machinery of the various republics.

Thus nationalism is to be brought down from its supremacy and absoluteness to be the servant of a supra-national idea. It may be that in the future the Communist training of youth and of the masses will succeed in this aim; it may be that the course of history with its increasing synthesising of all countries will work in the same direction. But at present the old forces——"Pan-Russian chauvinism" and "local nationalism"——

still have life in them and power over the souls of
men. The Communist leaders themselves admit
that these nationalist forces not only exist but
grow in strength. Stalin said in his report of
progress to the sixteenth party congress in July
1930: "They do exist, and the important thing
is that they are growing. There can be no
doubt about that. This much is certain, that the
general atmosphere of the intensification of the
class struggle is bound to bring with it a certain
intensification of national friction, which is also
reflected in the Party."

The "Pan-Russian chauvinists" will have nothing to do with the efforts to promote and
encourage the national languages and cultures of
the small peoples. They regard the manifold
national autonomies as expensive in comparison
with a uniform centralism, and superfluous. From
the national standpoint they see in them a menace
to the unity of the Russian realm, a dissipation
of its internal energies and of its effectiveness
abroad. From the international standpoint they
see in them simply a "bourgeois fad." "Local
nationalism" is preached and promoted by all the
elements which for economic or social reasons
oppose the dictatorship of the proletariat and

aspire to secede from the Union and form "bourgeois" national states of their own. The Party combats both deviations from its own line, the Pan-Russian and the local alike, but it sees the principal danger in the Pan-Russian and not in the local movement, for the growth of Russian nationalism would be bound to produce by way of reaction a growth of local nationalism.

Those peoples of the Soviet Union which have an intelligentzia dating from pre-revolutionary times, and whose national consciousness has been strengthened through the encouragement which it has received from the Soviet Government, are agitating for state independence. Among the Ukrainians and the White Russians there are westernizing tendencies that object to a cultural dependence on Moscow and on the semi-Asiatic Soviet Union, and desire to follow the cultural models of the West, the latest currents of bourgeois literature and art. Among the Turco-Tartar peoples there are Pan-Turk and Pan-Islamic movements that have gained strength, and to this day there exists among them an urge towards independence that is probably stronger than among any other people of the Soviet Union. Right down to recent times the soviet authorities have been kept busy by a series of armed risings in central Asia. The liberty that the peoples of the Soviet Union have experienced in comparison with Tsarist times, and the spread of nationalism to Asia, have produced stronger emanations of the nationalist spirit than under Tsarism. Only the many backward populations of the Soviet Union—populations of no great numerical importance or with no considerable territory, who suffered neglect or persecution under Tsarist rule, saw their lands confiscated, and seemed doomed to gradual extinction through alcohol and disease—can be unreservedly grateful for the nationality policy of the Soviet Government. Among these "pre-national" tribes the Government had nothing to destroy, had only to build up.[22]

Among the more highly developed peoples of the Union, which had already experienced the influence of Europe and its nationalism, which had already a record of cultural achievements and had their own traditions, the scope allowed to their national energies by Communism is insufficient to satisfy their national ambitions. So the struggle continues between the forward-looking rationalism of Communism and the ebullitions of nationalism under the influences of the past. But if the class struggle that replaces the national struggle is carried on with the same bitterness and the same belief in force and terrorism with which national struggles are carried on in Europe, it has nevertheless another aspect: it aims at preparing the way for a classless society, a warless age of peace, while nationalism holds out no hope, even in theory, of being able to produce a peaceful human society through the dissolution of other nations and their merging into one all-embracing nation in the course of the historic process. Socialism is characterized by a universal human aim of which nationalism by its very nature is incapable, for all that the ill-defined thinking of a Liberal epoch sought to hold it up as a vague hope.

Will Communism succeed in filling the peoples of the great Eurasian subcontinent, from the eastern slopes of the Carpathians to the Pacific Ocean and from the Arctic Ocean to the Hindu-Kush, with a common will, a new way of living, a single economic doctrine? But Communism aspires to yet more. In the words of the declaration which accompanied its creation, the Soviet Union is intended to be "a new and decisive step

along the road to the union of the workers of all
countries in the Socialist World Soviet Republic."
The banner of the Union dispenses with all
national emblems.   The beasts of prey of the
state, lions, eagles, bears, are of no more concern
to it than their noble and world-shaking counter-
part, the paradox of the lamb.   It shows as
symbols of the new evangel of world-wide labour
a sickle and hammer on a sunlit globe framed in
ears of corn.   Interwoven with the ears are
ribbons bearing in various languages the device,
"Proletarians of all countries, unite!"   In this
urge towards a united and peaceful humanity,
towards the removal of the dissensions and differences of races and nations and classes, there
appears once more an old spiritual heritage of
humanity, which in the last resort is just as
irrational in origin and as deeply rooted in men's
bones as the substance and consciousness of
race and the historical traditionalism of nations.
It has come into the clear vision of men's intelligence and has been the goal of their efforts at
turning-points of history; in the passions of the
struggle for power between groupings determined by blood-relationship and fate, men have
again and again been able to forsake it, but

always they have come back to it.   Marx too was
inspired by this ancient evangel, born of man's
intelligence and his instinctive aspirations.   He
preached it as a disciple of the age of rationalism
and its humanism.   In doing so he took up his
position in an age-long procession—the witness
to their faith of the prophets and the early Chris-
tians, the hopes of the ancient world of which the
last echoes were heard in the Stoa, and those of
Young Europe as it awoke in rationalism to full
consciousness.   And with this message yet another
ancient dream and evangel has united in the Russian soul, that of Slavophil Messianism, in which
Russia appears as the protagonist and apostle, the
suffering demonstrator and interpreter of the
meaning of human history.   Just as territorial
conditions continue to operate in the policy of the
Soviet Union that had before determined the
policy of the Tsarist empire, so there continue to
operate in Bolshevism fundamental characteristics of the ethnical groups which are putting it
into practice.

The Soviet Government realized from the first
the importance of the question of nationality to
the economic organization of its territories.   The
great Eurasian plains and steppes demanded a

vast economic synthesis. To allow these territories to be split up into independent national
states would have been fatal in more than a merely
economic respect. The areas tilled by the various
peoples were in many cases dotted about among
one another and deeply indented into one another;
many were too small to be able to survive as
economic units. New national states would have
attempted in their ambition for power to extend
their territories at the expense of their neighbours,
as happened in Transcaucasia from 1918 to 1920.
What was needed was a constitutional formula
which would enable the single vast economic
area to be inhabited by many peoples on equal
terms. A break had to be made with the fundamental theory of the modern national state, *cuius
regio, illius ratio*. Every attempt to divest the
members of the non-Russian peoples of their
national rights, to deprive them of full opportunities of education or of access to administrative
and economic official posts, to undermine their
economic position, had to be eschewed.

Such were the basic principles underlying the
nationality policy of the Soviet Union. It
established full equality of rights between all its
peoples. It brought them freedom to develop

their own language, and self-government in a measure unknown before. It was careful to avoid hurting their national susceptibilities or by any sort of oppression awakening nationalist reaction. Communism realizes and recognizes the multiplicity and variety of peoples, and is aware that even after the building up of Socialism has been completed they will endure for a long period all over the world. It tries to secure peace between the peoples, and to meet their national needs and aspirations so far as is compatible with the execution of its Socialist programme. This limit, it is true, is so narrow that it is impossible to speak of any "liberty" of the nations of the Union. The Soviet Government is not Russian but proletarian, it does not seek to Russify the peoples of the Union but to train them as Communists like the Russian people itself, partners in the building up of Socialism. This training is undertaken with all the resources of the state, and in it lies the means of ending the conflict between Communism and nationalism. For in the last resort there can be no compromise. Two conceptions of the meaning of history are here face to face, the myth of nationalism, dating from the eighteenth and nineteenth centuries, and a new myth, the roots of which go down deep into the past, but which is being propagated by means of a new social message. Will the new myth of Universalism be able to transform the type of humanity that has evolved in the last two centuries? Will the world-wide economic interdependence and the annihilation of distance, entirely unknown in past centuries, pull down the barriers between the peoples; will a common distress and a common task produce a realization of the common basis of the life of all men?

Outside the Soviet Union, Socialism has as yet proved powerless as a supra-national force. Nationalism has won the day, has shown itself the stronger force and the one more closely in touch with men's lives; in recent years it has made important advances in the extension of its sphere of influence and in the consolidation of its power. Only in the Soviet Union does the national question fail to dominate state policy and public life as it does in other countries; alongside the tasks of the building up of Socialism and the forming of the new type of humanity it is falling from its place of pride into the background. Whether new forces are to mould human history and determine the form of human society, will

I

depend on the success or failure of the building up of Socialism and the forming of the new type of humanity.

Thus in considering every particular aspect of the Communist programme one is driven back again and again to the fundamental question of the realization of Communism as a whole. It cannot be otherwise with Communism, as an ordering of life that takes account of all life, and aims at interpreting its meaning by a universalistic and all-embracing conception of the history and destiny of mankind.

NOTES

[1] In 1917 there was 5,400,000,000 roubles of foreign capital invested in state and municipal loans in Russia and 2,200,000,000 in Russian industries. The foreign participation in the capital of the Russian iron and steel industry was 90 per cent, in the petroleum industry 87 per cent, and so on. The Russian Empire was thus a "colony" of Western Capitalism. Communism has set out entirely to alter all this. The 14th Communist Party Congress, which adopted the policy of the industrialization of the Union, did so "in order that the U.S.S.R. may be converted from a country which imports machinery and apparatus into one which produces its own machinery and equipment, so that the Soviet Union shall not become in any event an economic appendage of capitalist world trade and industry, but shall grow into an independent economic unit." The further phrase "which is being socialistically built up" is of no particular importance in this connexion. Characteristic in this regard is the attitude of a patriotic section of the Russian anti-Communist *émigrés*, who have recognized that Bolshevism signifies the "national" liberation of Russia from the domination of foreign Imperialism. See Prince D. S. Mirsky, "Histoire d'une Emancipation," in the *Nouvelle Revue Française* of September 1, 1931. He writes of the Eurasians (p. 386): "This movement was outspokenly xenophobe and anti-West. It was a nationalism of the type that forms in subject races, for it was clear that a non-Bolshevist Russia could only be a colony of western

Imperialism, and that the Communists have saved Russia from colonial slavery. Eurasianism may be described as a Russian Gandhism."

2 It is especially this attitude of the Soviet Union that has been a model for the other "eastern" countries, in so far as they had an educated intelligentzia of the modern type. Let two examples suffice here: Dr. Sun Yat-sen and his circle in China, and the Peruvian Jose Carlos Mariategui, who died, a young man, in 1930 as a leader of his generation; in open admiration and emulation of the U.S.S.R. he demanded industrialization for South America (see Waldo Frank, *America Hispana*, New York 1931, pp. 166–177). For China's industrialization see also Ernst Rüdenberg, *Zur Entwicklung von Chinas Wirtschaft und Politik*, Kurt Vowinckel Verlag, Berlin 1932.

3 As an example of the awakening of the active co-operation of the masses in every field, mention may be made of the invitations made in the famous art gallery of the Leningrad Hermitage to the workers to co-operate by criticism, questions, and proposals in improving the arrangement of the pictures and the clarity of the comments on them; stamped addressed envelopes are provided for this purpose. In the Historical Museum in Moscow, in the halls not yet arranged from Marxist standpoints, the workers who visit the museum are invited to make suggestions for the best way of altering the old arrangement from the new points of view; the difference between the various methods of arrangement are made clear by graphic representations. Everywhere the effort is plain to give the masses the feeling of co-operation and of joint responsibility, to seek their advice, and to produce the closest possible contact between science and the people, research and life.

⁴ The object of the Constitution of the R.S.F.S.R. is, according to Article 1, "to guarantee the dictatorship of the proletariat for the purpose of suppressing the bourgeoisie, of abolishing the exploitation of man by man, and of bringing about Communism, under which there will be neither division into classes nor state power." Under Marxism the bearer of this historic mission is the industrial proletariat. Lenin concludes from that that "The true and only basis for the setting up of a Socialist society is simply and purely the heavy industry." The class dominance of the proletariat is to lead to the classless society, that is to the existence of the single class of the proletariat. With the carrying into effect of the dominance of the proletariat on a world-wide scale the state itself disappears. Even for the transition period Lenin postulates "the carrying out of all duties of the state, free of cost, by the worker who has completed his eight hours of work in the factory." The "new mass form of workers' control from below" will serve as preparation for this—the taking over of control of a department of state, an economic organization, or an institution by the workers of a particular factory.

⁵ Marx himself has pointed out that the communal constitution of the Paris Commune, which served as a model for the soviets, "would have brought the rural producers under the intellectual leadership of the chief towns of the districts, and would have assured them there of the natural representatives of their interests in the town workers." In the Marxist view economic progress leads through the decay of the peasantry to the machine-run large-scale farm, which produces more and more remuneratively. "The capitalist large farm will inflict discomfiture on their (the peasants') feeble and obsolete

farming, with as much ease as the railway discomfited the cart." (Friedrich Engels.)

[6] The fight against the general setting up of money as the criterion of value is also being carried on, on another plane, by the traditional East, to which pre-revolutionary Russia belonged, and which is represented to-day principally by Gandhi and India. Gandhi has identified himself completely with the poverty of India, and his way of living is a formidable challenge to the criteria of value which determined the attitude of men in the West, a challenge similar to that of Communism, whose leaders also, as representatives of the masses, live the life of the masses. But while the two protests agree in rejecting the positive criteria of value applied by the West, Communism aims at a general overcoming of poverty, at the assurance of an economically and technically adequate standard of life to be enjoyed by everyone through the allocation to him of the full yield of his labour—whereas in the Indian view poverty is not only a natural but a legitimate and often a holy state of life, and a raising of the standard of the externals of life by technique and hygiene is inessential.

[7] Officially, in its Constitution, the Soviet state preserves neutrality in the struggle between church and state; but the combating of religion is one of the tasks of the Communist Party. The party programme of 1919 contains the following passage: "In regard to religion the Party does not content itself with the separation of state and church and of school and church—measures which appear in the programmes of the bourgeois democracy, but, in consequence of the bonds which in reality unite capital and religious propaganda, are nowhere carried by it to completion. The Party is guided by the conviction

that only the achievement of a planned and deliberate
ordering of the whole of the economic activities of the
masses will result in the entire dying out of religious
prejudices. . . . In anti-religious propaganda care must
be taken to avoid any hurt to the feelings of believers,
as this leads to the hardening of religious fanaticism."
This last sentence (unlike the similar provision in regard
to propaganda against nationalism, which is observed
with the utmost care in such propaganda) was soon dis-
regarded in anti-religious propaganda, when the Communists found that the religious feelings of the masses were
more easily got rid of than they had expected. No legal
obstacle is set in the way of the conduct of religious
services in churches or homes, but religious instruction
of persons under eighteen is prohibited, and the complete
separation of church from state has robbed many churches
and priests of their means of existence, especially as the
priests have lost the rights of citizenship.   If the majority
of the believers propose that a church or synagogue or
mosque shall be closed and are no longer prepared to
maintain it, it is turned into a workers' club or a museum
or welfare institution.

The social and economic policy of the soviets produced
bitter opposition, and their nationality policy was the
subject of hot controversy; but their anti-religious policy
has met with scarcely any serious opposition. The youth
of all religions have apparently been won for "atheism."
The Soviet youth dispense with religion as a matter of
course.   The question whether there is a God or not
is considered to have been solved long ago for every
" enlightened, modern, scientifically educated" person.
Even among most of the older Russian peasants, the
indifference is astonishing; their supposed ecstasy of faith

has not withstood the promptings of their primitive, shrewd, calculating nature. The god of the gorgeous altars was taken for a miracle-worker and was understood to be an ally of the Tsar's. Now the Tsar is gone, the miracle-working ikons and the powerful priests have fallen, and God has not wiped the evil-doers off the face of the earth.—Only the women show more loyalty to the fallen church.

[8] The Union of the Godless enjoys the sympathy of the authorities, but is not an official body. One does not get the impression that it has any great vitality or does any very active work except in the weeks preceding the great religious festivals. There is a weekly journal, *The Godless*, and a periodical of the same name that appears at very irregular intervals. Both make a poor show; their propaganda is often absurd and tasteless, and sometimes of a disarming naiveté in face of the depths of the religious problem. The Union has 3,500,000 members. In its own five-year plan it set out to secure 17,000,000 members in 1933. But it admits that this "will remain a mere paper proposal." As to its national composition, it gives the following figures: 460,000 Ukrainians, 40,000 White Russians, 200,000 Jews, 45,000 Tartars, 20,000 Bashkirs, 25,000 Uzbeks, 5000 Azerbaijan Turks, 3000 Kazaks, 5000 Tchuvash, 1500 Turcomans, 1500 Kirghiz.

Much more effective is the propaganda against religion with which the whole of the educative work of the Soviet is saturated. It is at its most effective where it is not pursued in isolation but fitted into the whole system of life and education. Past history is viewed from this new standpoint. In the most beautiful of the old Russian churches, the church erected in the Red Square in Moscow by Ivan IV as a thank-offering for the conquest of Kazan, striking diagrams demonstrate that the war against Kazan was not undertaken as a god-fearing work which deserved the church's blessing, but was an imperialistic war waged in the interests of the rich Moscow merchants. The oppression of women under theocratic rule is contrasted again and again with their emancipation by Socialism. The war between Christianity and paganism in eleventh-century Russia is represented as a class war, with the princes on the side of Christianity. In the museums many early documents, with translations and comments, describe the oppression of the peasants in the past by the church and the nobles, and the bitter want which the peasants suffered through the alliance of these powers.

[9] The higher educational institutions in the Soviet Union are intended for the training of the economic and technical leaders drawn from the new ruling class of the working masses, who in the past were shut out from secondary and university education. Accordingly, the children of the so-called Lishentzi, members of the former ruling class now deprived of political rights, are excluded from attendance at the higher educational institutions. They can secure the right to attend, however, by publicly dissociating themselves from their parents.

[10] This element of anonymity is to be found also in the leadership. The leading men in the Soviet Union have no biography, no private life. The Communist press never publishes news concerning Stalin's family life, never shows pictures of his children. It is this complete exclusion of every private element that distinguishes the Communist press so sharply from the American and also

from the European press. All that is known of the leader is the party offices which he has held. In his habits Stalin identifies himself with the Party; he retires behind the will of the Party though he forms it; outwardly he is always simply a bit of the Party. Lenin, Stalin, and all the other leaders dress and live like the masses whom they represent, the proletariat in whose name they speak, much as Gandhi in his habits and his clothing represents in externals the poverty of the masses of India in whose name he speaks.

Since his death Lenin has become the "saint" of Communism, his portrait has replaced the ikons, the old saints' pictures; but this has nothing to do with Lenin the individual or with any private biography of the type which has become so popular in western Europe, but only with the party leader and his public life. The completeness of Stalin's victory over Trotzky is to be explained by the fact that Trotzky had not enough anonymity, was too much of the individualist intellectual, too little of the typical, average man in whom the masses could recognize their own image, had too much intellectual superiority.

11 Communism has much the same relationship to nationalism as the other great mediæval faiths, Catholicism and Islam, both of which are non-national or supranational in principle. Islam was always an enemy of pride of race or national prejudices: the Mohammedan of whatever colour or origin was the equal of every other Mohammedan; Catholicism insisted equally, at least in principle, on the equality of all races. Modern racial arrogance, the colour bar, which conflict with the Christian principle that all are the children of God, first made their appearance with northern Protestantism,

That creed came into the world at the beginning of the era of nationalism, and actively spread the secular theory of the separation of the spheres of religion and politics (the true religious theory demands man's whole and undivided allegiance); thus, especially in Germany, it became more and more the theology of nationalism. On occasion it served in Britain and the United States to justify on "religious" and "biblical" grounds the treatment meted out to negroes, Indians, and coloured or "inferior" races in general.

[12] Even in times of political tension, when the Soviet press is attacking the policy of foreign governments, the British, for instance, or the French, care is always taken to avoid exciting national hatred or chauvinism; it is always pointed out that there is no quarrel with the foreign nation but only with its government, which is opposed by sections of the nation, for instance the proletariat.

[13] For the eastern policy of the Soviet Government, see the chapter on the subject in Hans Kohn: *A History of Nationalism in the East* (Routledge, 1929).

[14] A connecting link between the direct influence of Communism on the eastern peoples within the Soviet Union and the indirect and much smaller influence on the other eastern peoples is formed by the two central Asiatic People's Republics of Tannu-Tuva and the more important Mongolia, which are outside the Soviet Union but are associated with it in many ways. The proselytizing influence of a religion coming from without can especially be studied among the Mongols. This race brought all Asia and half Europe under their yoke under Genghis Khan in the twelfth century. In the sixteenth century, through the adoption of Lamaist Buddhism, their old

spirit was completely broken and they were turned into peaceful and pious men. According to the census of 1918, 45 per cent of the population were monks. The influence of the Communist Revolution has now worked on them in the opposite direction. In this the Soviet Government has had the advantage of the circumstance that it has within its frontiers two Buddhist Mongol peoples, the Buriats and the Kalmuks, so that the Communist training of these peoples exercised a propagandist influence beyond the frontiers. A strong opponent of Communism, Iwan Jakowlewitsch Korostovetz, writes in his book *Von Cinggis Khan zur Sowjetrepublik* (Walter de Gruyter, Berlin 1926), p. 90: "The revolutionary propaganda had awakened the national consciousness of the Mongols, but had also, at the same time, awakened the wild instincts of this race, which until then had been held in check by social and religious inhibitions that had endured for centuries." There is another aspect of the process: the Soviet Government is using the Mongol People's Republic to gain influence over other Mongol peoples. The Constitution of the Mongol People's Republic of November 26, 1924, opens with a "Declaration of Rights of the Workers of Mongolia," which runs as follows: "Mongolia is hereby declared to be an independent republic, in which the whole power belongs to the workers. The people exercise their supreme authority through the Grand Huruldan of the entire people and through the Government elected thereby. The fundamental task of the Mongolian Republic consists in the destruction of the remnants of the feudal theocratic system and in the consolidation of the new republican order on the basis of the complete democratization of the administration of the state."

[15] The Autonomous Socialist Soviet Republic of the Volga Germans has 631,300 inhabitants; of these, 66·4 per cent are Germans, 20·4 per cent Russians, 12 per cent Ukrainians. The republic is divided into twelve cantons; in six of these the language is German, in two German and Russian, in two German and Ukrainian, and in two German, Russian, and Ukrainian. The capital of the republic, formerly known as Pokrovsk, has been renamed Engels. The old capital was formerly called Katharinenstadt, because the German colonists originally came into the country under Catherine II in 1764; after the Revolution it was renamed Marxstadt. In the Presidium of the Central Executive Committee of the republic there are seven Germans and four Russians. The nationality law of the Republic of the Volga Germans is described in two publications in German, which also give a valuable account of the general nationality policy of the Soviet Government—Rudolf Schilze-Mölkau, *Die Grundzüge des wolgadeutschen Staatswesens im Rahmen der russischen Nationalitätenpolitik*, Verlag Ernst Reinhardt, Munich 1931, and especially Manfred Langhans-Ratzeburg, *Die Wolgadeutschen, Ihr Staats- und Verwaltungsrecht in Vergangenheit und Gegenwart, zugleich ein Beitrag zum bolschewistischen Nationalitätenrecht*, Ost-Europa-Verlag, Berlin 1929.

[16] The number of workers organized in trade unions in 1929 in the Ukraine was 1,767,411. Of these 56·86 per cent were Ukrainians by nationality, 25·41 per cent Russians, 11·79 per cent Jews, 1·74 per cent Poles; the language percentages were 43·26 Ukrainian, 49·83 Russian, 4·85 Yiddish, and 0·61 Polish. In White Russia there were 247,447 workers organized in trade unions, of whom 63·98 per cent were

White Russians, 24·72 per cent Jews, 5·93 per cent Russians, and 2·82 per cent Poles. In Armenia there were 58,461 organized workers, 89·41 per cent being Armenians. In Azerbaijan, which includes Baku, there were 214,670 workers organized in trade unions in July 1928 ; 38·1 per cent were Azerbaijan Turks, 36·5 per cent Russians, and 15·5 per cent Armenians. In Uzbekistan in 1929 there were 142,163 organized workers, including 56·47 per cent Russians and 26·29 per cent Uzbeks. The proportion was similar in Turkmenistan—59·35 per cent Russians, 22·66 Turcomans.

[17] The Turksib is also of great importance for the future penetration of Chinese Turkestan and for the building of the great land route from Europe to China. The vast north-western outer areas of the Chinese Republic, economically virgin territory, are a region full of promise for the Soviet Union, as Outer Mongolia and Tannu-Tuva already show.

[18] The *Journal of the Royal Institute of International Affairs* for July 1928 publishes a report by Prince Lobanov-Rostovsky on "The Soviet Muslim Republics in Central Asia," in the course of which he writes (pp. 247-8, 250):

"As a result of all these violent perturbations the social structure of Russian Central Asia had undergone important modifications. The power of the native rulers, the Muslim clergy and the feudal chieftains, the *begs*, had now been broken. The curious mediæval guilds which had controlled the trades in the cities had disappeared. Thus the whole framework of a social order was done away with by one formidable blow. A Soviet ethnographical expedition reported the disappearance of public worship, of old traditions and, most important of all, of the

clan spirit among the natives. Curiously (?) enough, the
expedition reported an increase of national, or more
exactly racial, feeling amongst the natives. . . . It is
curious (?) to notice that in their attempt to stamp out
dynastic, religious, or clan traditions which are so strong
in Asia, the Soviets are not afraid to foster an entirely
embryonic nationalism. In this they show a real insight
into the native character, and to any objection which
may be raised they can always say, not without irony,
that they have given the natives more by substituting a
racial unity for a State unity."

[19] The following figures, for 1930, may be given in
regard to education in the national republics. In the
Armenian S.S.R. 1316 students were attending the
university, 98·4 per cent being Armenians. The following were the numbers attending the higher professional
colleges, the so-called Technika:

Colleges.	Students.	Percentage of Armenians.	Turks
Teachers' training	. 2,034	85·94	14·06
Labour faculties	. 790	90·76	8·61
Trade . .	. 515	99·81	—
Agricultural .	. 415	91·57	8·43
Social-economic .	. 142	99·29	—
Music and art .	. 146	97·95	—

The figures for the beginning of the school year 1929–
1930 in the Turkmenistan S.S.R. were:

| | | Percentage of | |
Colleges.	Students.	Turco-mans.	Uzbeks.	Russians and other Europeans.
Teachers' training	1,878	70·77	11·87	2·29
Labour faculties .	367	40·87	3·27	46·05
Agricultural .	1,446	36·45	2·90	45·79
Industrial . .	356	38·76	—	45·79
Medical . .	416	14·18	4·33	62·26
Accountancy .	197	84·77	4·06	—

As regards the education of girls, the proportion of girls attending to the total numbers attending school in Transcaucasia was 41·4 per cent in the case of the Georgians, 36·6 per cent among the Armenians, and 17·2 per cent among the Azerbaijan Turks; in Uzbekistan 13·7 per cent of the Uzbek school children were girls, and in Turkmenistan 7·1 per cent of the Turcoman children. In the R.S.F.S.R. the percentage of girls among the elementary school children was—Russian, 40·2; Tartar, 41·2; German, 46; and Jew, 49·4.

The books published in the Azerbaijan S.S.R. in 1929 were as follows:

	Books and pamphlets published.	Total No. of copies.	Total No. of sheets.
Total issue . .	997	2,981,685	13,107,642
Issued in Azerbaijan Turkish .	568	2,053,916	9,429,944
In Azerbaijan, Turkish and Russian .	46	104,935	252,085
In Russian . .	350	743,125	3,227,137

In the Turkmenistan S.S.R. there appeared in the first nine months of 1929 68 works in Turcoman, of which 267,170 copies were issued containing 1,179,226 sheets, and 37 in Russian, of which 85,550 copies were issued containing 684,783 sheets.

[20] In addition to the publishing institutions in the various national republics and autonomous regions a central Publishing Office for the Peoples of the U.S.S.R. was at work in Moscow, engaged entirely on books in other languages than Russian, especially in the languages of those peoples, such as Poles, Chinese, gypsies, and others, who had no territories of their own in the U.S.S.R. In January 1931, for instance, this office issued the following publications in the language of the Mari: A reading book, *Our past. A reading book in sociology for the first grade schools.* It was issued in an edition of 4000 copies, and its 104 pages described the life of the peasants and workers in pre-revolutionary times and the history of the Revolution. An edition of 5000 copies of *Unified Programme* for semi-illiterates and 8000 copies for entire illiterates, for use in the instruction of adults in the schools for the liquidation of illiteracy. Pamphlets on the carrying out of the election campaign in 1930–1931 in the national areas, on the liquidation of the kulak class, on the carrying out of the industrial and financial plan and the Socialist reconstruction of agriculture, and on the proceedings of the 16th Communist Party Congress. The anti-religious propaganda publications were a pamphlet, "Who has any need of Christmas festivals?" and a stage play, "The Mask," on the alliance between priests and kulaks. In addition, five educational works on agriculture were issued. The bulk of the publications were in German, Tartar, and Tchuvash.

K

21 The Soviet Government has followed the example of Peter the Great in simplifying the Russian alphabet. The Hebrew alphabet, in which the Yiddish language is written, has also been simplified, phonetic considerations being taken into account, as in Russian, instead of historic ones.

22 It is also possible to study in Moscow an example of Soviet work among primitive peoples. As in Hungary and other countries, there are gypsies in the Soviet Union, who live there as elsewhere on various arts, together with begging and horse-stealing. In Moscow there live some 4000 members of this ancient and mysterious nomad race. In other countries they are left to themselves; the Soviet Government has formed a club from among the few active elements in the gypsy youth; it is called, in the gypsy language, "Red Star." It has some 700 members, of whom until quite recently only about 5 per cent could read and write. It is active in the liquidation of illiteracy, arranges lectures, organizes excursions to factories and museums, and issues the first wall newspaper in the gypsy language. Alongside this cultural activity an attempt is being made at the economic reorganization of gypsy life. The gypsies have been given land. Under the leadership of the Moscow club 7000 gypsy families have been settled on holdings; workshops have been started; and an obstinate struggle has begun against the past way of life of the gypsies. In harmony with the efforts of the Soviet Government on behalf of national cultures, the popular gypsy songs and dances have been developed and freed from the elements which had been interpolated in them through performance in places of entertainment. The first play staged by the club in the gypsy language dealt with the transition to a settled life.

APPENDIX I

THE BASES OF THE NATIONALITY POLICY OF THE COMMUNIST PARTY

1. From Stalin's *Marxism and the national question* (January 1913).
2. Resolution of the Petrograd Conference, April 1917.
3. Lenin's concluding speech at the eighth Party Congress, March 1919.
4. From the programme of the Russian Communist Party.
5. From the theses on national and colonial questions of the Second Congress of the Communist International, July 1920.
6. From the Constitution of the U.S.S.R. (1923) and of the R.S.F.S.R. (May 1925).
7. From Stalin's speech at the sixteenth Party Congress (July 1930).

FROM A PAMPHLET OF STALIN'S "MARXISM AND THE NATIONAL QUESTION" (JANUARY 1913)

. . . At this difficult moment a high mission falls upon the Social Democracy—to take up its position against nationalism, to keep the masses out of the general current. The Social Democracy and it alone can do this, by opposing to nationalism the proven weapon of internationalism, the

unity and indivisibility of the class struggle. The higher
the wave of nationalism rises, the more loudly must the
voice of the Social Democracy be raised for the fraternity
and unity of the proletarians of all nationalities of
Russia. . . .

That is why the workers are fighting and will fight
against every policy of national oppression in all its forms,
from the subtlest to the crudest. That is why the Social
Democracy of all countries is proclaiming the right of the
peoples to self-determination. The right of self-determination means that only the nation itself has the right to
determine its fate, that no one has the right forcibly to
intervene in the life of the nation, to destroy its schools
and other institutions, to break down its customs and
usages, to oppress its language, to cut down its rights.

Naturally that does not mean that the Social Democracy
will support any and every usage and institution of the
nation's. It will battle against the violation of nations,
it will defend the right of the nation itself to determine its
destiny, but at the same time it will lead an agitation
against harmful usages and institutions of such a nation,
in order to give the working classes the opportunity of
liberating themselves from them.

The right of self-determination means that the nation
may order its life according to its own desires. . . . The
nation is sovereign, and all nations have equal rights.
That does not, of course, mean that the Social Democracy
will defend every demand of the nations. The nation
has even the right to turn back to old conditions, but that
does not mean that the Social Democracy agrees to that.
The duty of the Social Democracy, which defends the
interests of the proletariat, and the rights of the nation,
which consists of various classes, are two different things.

In fighting for the national right of self-determination, the Social Democracy intends to make an end of the national policy of oppression, to make it impossible, and so to undermine the national struggle, to rob it of its sting, and to reduce it to a minimum. In this way the policy of the class-conscious proletariat is sharply distinguished from that of the bourgeoisie, which aims at intensifying the nationalist struggle and continuing and redoubling the nationalist agitation. . . .

The nation has the right freely to determine its destiny. . . . It has the right of secession. But that does not mean that it must do this under all circumstances, that autonomy or separation will always and everywhere be advantageous to the nation, that is to its majority, that is to the working classes. . . . All these are questions of which the solution depends on the concrete historical conditions . . . which, like everything else, change, so that decisions which at a given moment are right may appear entirely inacceptable at another moment.

RESOLUTION OF THE PETROGRAD CITY AND ALL-RUSSIAN CONFERENCE OF THE RUSSIAN SOCIAL DEMOCRATIC LABOUR PARTY (BOLSHEVIKI) ON THE NATIONAL QUESTION (APRIL 1917).

The policy of national oppression, an inheritance from autocracy and monarchy, is maintained by the land-owners, the capitalists, and the petty bourgeoisie for the sake of the protection of their class interests and the division of the workers of the various populations. Present-day Imperialism, which reinforces the effort to bring weak peoples into subjection, appears as a new factor in the intensification of national oppression.

In so far as national oppression can be got rid of in capitalist society, it can be only through a steadily-pursued democratic and republican ordering and administration of the state, assuring full equality of rights to all nations and languages.

All nations within Russia must be accorded the right freely to secede and to form independent states. The denial of this right, and the failure to adopt measures guaranteeing its practical realization, amount to the support of a policy of conquests and annexations. Only the recognition by the proletariat of the right of nations to secession assures the complete solidarity of the workers of the various nations and makes possible a true democratic coming together of the nations. The struggle which has broken out between Finland and the Russian Government for the time being shows plainly that the denial of freedom to secede leads to a direct continuation of the policy of Tsarism.

The question of the right of nations freely to secede is unjustifiably confused with the question of the expediency of the secession of one or another nation at one or another moment. This latter question must in each separate instance be determined in entire independence by a party of the proletariat, from the point of view of the interests of general development and of the proletarian class struggle for Socialism.

The Party demands a broad territorial autonomy . . . the abolition of the compulsory use of the official language, and the determination of the boundaries of the self-governing and autonomous districts on the basis of the economic conditions and conditions of existence as taken into account by the local population itself, of the national composition of the population, and so on.

The Party entirely rejects so-called cultural national autonomy, that is, the turning over of education and similar institutions from state administration to the special national Parliaments. National cultural autonomy divides the workers living in a district, and even those working in the same enterprises, artificially according to their membership of this or that "national culture"; that is, it strengthens the bond between the workers and the bourgeois culture of the various nations, while the task of the Social Democracy consists in the strengthening of the international culture of the world proletariat.

The Party demands the incorporation in the Constitution of a fundamental law declaring invalid every sort of privilege of any nation and every sort of limitation of the rights of national minorities.

The interests of the working class demand the association of the workers of all the nationalities of Russia in uniform proletarian organizations, political, trade union, co-operative, and so on. Only such association of the workers of the various nationalities in uniform organizations enables the proletariat to carry on a successful struggle with international capital and with bourgeois nationalism.

(Adopted by 56 votes to 16, with 18 abstentions.)

FROM LENIN'S CONCLUDING SPEECH AT THE EIGHTH CONGRESS OF THE RUSSIAN COMMUNIST PARTY, DELIVERED ON MARCH 19, 1919.

. . . It seems to me that the Finnish example and that of the Bashkirs show that in the question of nationality it is not possible to proceed from the assumption that economic unity is necessary at any price. Necessary, of course, it is. But we must attain it through propaganda, through agitation, through a voluntary union. The Bashkirs distrust the Russians, because the Russians are at a higher level of civilization and have used their civilization to rob the Bashkirs. Consequently in these remote districts the name Russian means "oppressor" to the Bashkirs. . . . We must take that into account, we must combat it. But that takes a long time. It is not to be got rid of by a decree. We must go to work on this very cautiously. Above all such a nation as the Russians, who have excited a wild hatred in all other nations, must be particularly cautious. We have only now learnt to manage better, and even that only some of us as yet. Thus there are Communists among us who say "uniform schools," and accordingly no instruction to be given except through the Russian language. In my view a Communist who thinks in this way is a Pan-Russian chauvinist. This tendency still exists in many of us, and we must wrestle with it.

Consequently we must say to the other peoples that we are internationalists through and through, and are striving for a voluntary union of the workers and peasants of all nations. That does not by any means rule out wars. War is another question, following from the nature of Imperialism. If we are to fight Wilson, and Wilson turns a small nation into his tool, then we shall fight against this tool. . . . Under certain conditions a war may appear inevitable. But in the question of self-determination the position is that the various peoples proceed along the same historic course, but by very different circuitous routes and paths, and that nations at a higher level of civilization proceed of set purpose in a different way to those at a lower level. . . . If we were to leave this out of sight, we should be cutting the nationality question out of our programme. We could do so if men had no national characteristics. But men of that sort do not exist, and we can build up a Socialist society in no other way.

FROM THE PROGRAMME OF THE RUSSIAN COMMUNIST PARTY IN REGARD TO NATIONALITY POLICY

In the nationality question the Russian Communist Party is guided by the following principles:

1. It takes as starting-point the union of the proletarians and semi-proletarians of the various peoples for the common revolutionary struggle for the overthrow of the landowners and the bourgeoisie.

2. In order to overcome the suspicion felt by the working masses in the oppressed countries of the proletariat of the states that oppress these countries, all privileges of any sort of any national group whatever must be abolished, and the full equality of rights of nations, and the right of secession of colonies, and of nations with equal rights, must be recognized.

3. As a transitional form along the road to complete unity, the Party sets up the federative association of the states organized in the soviet form.

4. In the question who is the representative of the will of the nation at the moment of secession, the Russian Communist Party adopts the historic class standpoint. It takes account in that connexion of the degree of development of the nation in question—whether it is progressing from mediævalism to bourgeois democracy or from bourgeois democracy to the soviet or proletarian democracy, and so on.

In any case, there is needed on the part of the proletariat of the former ruling nations a special consideration and sensitiveness for the national feelings of the working masses of the oppressed nations, or nations without full rights. Only a policy of this sort can create the conditions for a really sincere and voluntary union of the various national elements of the international proletariat, as the experience of the union of a number of national soviet republics with Soviet Russia has shown.

FROM THE THESES DRAFTED BY LENIN ON THE NATION-
   ALITY AND COLONIAL QUESTIONS, AND ADOPTED AT
   THE SECOND CONGRESS OF THE COMMUNIST INTER-
   NATIONAL, AT THE END OF JULY 1920

. . . 3. The imperialistic war of 1914–1918, waged by both sides with the slogan of the liberation of peoples and the right of peoples to self-determination, has made thoroughly clear to all peoples and to the oppressed classes of the whole earth the mendacity of bourgeois democratic phrasemaking. This war has shown by the peace treaties of Brest Litovsk and Bucarest on one hand and of Versailles and St. Germain on the other how the victorious bourgeoisie has quite shamelessly fixed the national boundaries to its own economic advantage. . . .

4. From these considerations of principle it follows that the basis of the whole policy of the Comintern in the nationality and colonial question must be formed by the coming together of the proletariat and the working masses of all peoples for a simultaneous revolutionary struggle for the overthrow of the landed proprietors and the bourgeoisie. Only such a coming together can give assurance of victory over Capitalism, without which

victory national oppression and inequality cannot be destroyed.

5. The world political situation has now placed the dictatorship of the proletariat on the order of the day, and all events in world politics are inevitably grouped around a single central point—the struggle of the international bourgeoisie against the Russian Soviet Republic, which must gather around itself the Communist movements among the advanced workers of all countries and also all national liberation movements of colonies and oppressed peoples, who have become convinced through bitter experience that their salvation lies only in union with the revolutionary proletariat and in the victory of the Soviet Power over Imperialism.

6. Consequently it is not possible now to rest content with the mere recognition or proclamation of the coming together of the workers of all nations, but a policy must be carried on of the effectuation of the closest union of all nationalist and colonial liberation movements with Soviet Russia. The forms of this union must be determined by the development of the Communist movement in the proletariat of each country or of the bourgeois democratic liberation movement in backward countries or among backward peoples.

7. Federation reveals itself as a transitional form to the full unity of the workers of all peoples. . . .

9. In inter-state relations the nationality policy of the Comintern cannot be satisfied with the merely formal, purely rhetorical, practically entirely non-committal recognition of the equality of rights of the nations, such as is offered by the bourgeois democracy, both the openly bourgeois democracy and the pseudo-socialistic democracy of the Second International.

Not only must the continual infringements of the equality of rights of nations and of the guaranteed rights of minorities in all capitalist states be exposed in the whole propaganda of the Communist parties, in Parliament and out of it . . . but direct assistance must also be rendered to the revolutionary movements among the dependent nations or those without equal rights and in the colonies. Without this latter especially important condition, the struggle against the oppression of dependent nations and colonies remains . . . a mendacious phrase. . . .

12. The centuries-old oppression of colonial and weak peoples by the imperialist Powers has produced in the working masses of the oppressed countries not only embitterment, but suspicion of the oppressing nations as a whole, including the proletariat of these nations. . . . As this suspicion and the nationalist prejudices can only disappear after the extirpation of Imperialism and Capitalism in the leading countries and after a radical change in all the bases of the economic life of the. backward countries, the dying out of these prejudices can only proceed slowly. Consequently the Communist proletariat of all countries must behave with special consideration and special tenderness for the national feelings that still survive among the long-oppressed countries and peoples, and, in order to make this suspicion and the nationalist prejudices disappear as quickly as possible, must also be ready for definite concessions. Without a voluntary effort of the proletariat for union and unity, and later a similar effort of all the working masses of all countries and peoples of the whole world, the victory over Capitalism cannot be finally achieved.

2. European Capitalism draws its strength principally not from the industrial countries of Europe, but from its colonial possessions. For its continuance it requires the control over widespread colonial markets and an extensive field of exploitation. . . .

3. The surplus value received from the colonies is the main source of the resources of modern Capitalism. Only after this source has finally dried up will the European working class be able to destroy the capitalist order.

4. The secession of the colonies and the proletarian revolution at home will destroy Capitalism in Europe. Accordingly the Communist International . . . must keep in close contact with the revolutionary forces which are taking part at present in the shaking off of Imperialism in the politically and economically oppressed countries. For complete success the world revolution needs the simultaneous operation of both forces. For the leaders of the Second International . . . the world outside Europe had no existence. They failed to perceive the necessity of the co-operation of the revolutionary movement in Europe and in the other continents. . . .

6. Foreign Imperialism, imposed on the eastern peoples, has beyond question restricted their social and economic development and deprived them of the opportunity of attaining the level of civilization which Europe and America have attained thanks to the policy of Imperialism, which has endeavoured to hold up industrial development in the colonies; only quite lately has an indigenous proletariat in the true sense come into existence.

The indigenous crafts carried on in the homes were unable to compete with the centralized industries of the imperialist countries. Consequently the majority of the population were driven into agriculture and the export of raw materials. On the other hand the concentration of estates in the hands of great landowners continued, with a consequent large increase in the number of the landless peasants. The enormous majority of the population of these colonies is in a state of subjection. As a result of this policy the spirit of protest which exists potentially in the masses of the people finds expression only through the numerically small body of the bourgeois intelligentzia. The foreign domination steadily obstructs the free development of social life; consequently the shaking off of it must be the first step of the Revolution. Assistance in the shaking off of foreign domination thus does not signify any solidarization with the nationalist currents among the indigenous bourgeoisie, but only the opening of the way for the proletariat of the colonies to its liberation.

9. In the first stages the revolution in the colonies will not be communistic, but if it is led from the first by the Communist advanced guards, the revolutionary masses will be led, with the gradually growing revolutionary experience, along the true way to the attainment of the goal. It would be entirely mistaken to propose to solve the agrarian question on purely Communist principles.

FROM THE CONSTITUTION OF THE UNION OF SOVIET SOCIALIST REPUBLICS (U.S.S.R.)

Part I

Declaration concerning the formation of the Union of Soviet Socialist Republics

Since the formation of the soviet republics the countries of the world have split into two camps—the camp of Capitalism and the camp of Socialism.

There, in the camp of Capitalism, we find national animosities and inequality, colonial slavery and chauvinism, national oppression and pogroms, imperialist brutality and wars.

Here, in the camp of Socialism, there is mutual confidence and peace, national freedom and equality, and the fraternal collaboration of nations peacefully dwelling side by side.

The attempts of the capitalist world for decades past to solve the problem of nationalities by combining the free development of peoples with the system of exploitation of man by man have proved fruitless. On the contrary, the tangle of national antagonisms becomes more and more involved, threatening the very existence of Capitalism. The bourgeoisie has shown itself powerless to organize the collaboration of nations.

Only in the camp of the Soviets, only under the dictatorship of the proletariat which rallied around itself the majority of the population, has it become possible to abolish national oppression root and branch, to create the conditions engendering mutual confidence, and to lay the foundations of a fraternal collaboration of nations. . . .

Finally, the very structure of soviet power, international in its class essence, impels the toiling masses of the soviet republics to enter the path of union to form one Socialist family.

All these circumstances imperatively demand the unification of the soviet republics into a single federal state capable of securing the peoples against attacks from without and assuring them of domestic economic prosperity and freedom of national development.

The will of the peoples constituting the soviet republics which recently assembled in the congresses of their respective soviets and there unanimously decided to form the "Union of Soviet Socialist Republics," is a reliable guarantee that the Union is a voluntary association of peoples enjoying equal rights, that the right of each republic to secede from the Union is inviolable, that admission to the Union is open to all Socialist Soviet Republics whether now existing or hereafter to come into being, that the new federal state will prove itself a worthy pinnacle crowning the foundations laid as early as October 1917 to permit nations to dwell peacefully side by side in fraternal collaboration, that it will serve as a reliable bulwark against world Capitalism and will mark a new and decisive step towards uniting the workers of the world into a World Socialist Soviet Republic.

Part II

Treaty

3. The sovereignty of the Union republics shall be restricted only to the extent set forth in the present Constitution, which restrictions shall be confined to the subject-matters delegated to the jurisdiction of the Union. Except as so restricted, every Union republic shall enjoy the rights of an independent state. The Union of the Soviet Socialist Republics shall protect the sovereign rights of the Union republics.

4. Each Union republic shall retain its right freely to secede from the Union.

2. The Russian Socialist Federative Soviet Republic is a Socialist state of workers and peasants, built on the basis of a federation of the national Soviet Republics.

4. For the purpose of assuring real liberty of conscience to the workers, the church is separated from the state and the school from the church; and the right of all citizens to practise freely any religious belief or to engage in anti-religious propaganda remains inviolate.

9. The Russian Socialist Federative Soviet Republic regards labour as an obligation for all citizens of the Republic.

11. The Russian Socialist Federative Soviet Republic extends all the rights granted under the Constitution and the legislative acts of the Republic to the citizens of the Russian Socialist Federative Soviet Republic, also to all citizens of the other Soviet Union republics residing within the territory of the R.S.F.S.R.

In view of its solidarity with the workers of all nations, the Russian Socialist Federative Soviet Republic grants all political rights to foreigners residing in the territory of the Russian Socialist Federative Soviet Republic for the purpose of engaging in productive labour, who belong to the working class, and to peasants who do not employ the labour of others, in accordance with the decisions of the supreme authorities of the Union of Soviet Socialist Republics.

12. The Russian Socialist Federative Soviet Republic grants the right of asylum to all foreigners persecuted for their revolutionary or liberating activities.

L

13. All citizens shall be equal before the law, irrespective of race or nationality. In conformity with this principle, the Russian Socialist Federative Soviet Republic declares all oppression of national minorities of whatever description and all disabilities whatsoever imposed on them, as well as the establishment or toleration of any direct or indirect special privileges for individual nationalities, to be absolutely incompatible with the fundamental laws of the Republic; the Russian Socialist Federative Soviet Republic recognizes the right of all its citizens freely to use their native language at Congresses, in courts of law, in the schools, in the administrative offices and in public life, and secures them in the full enjoyment of this right.

FROM STALIN'S POLITICAL REPORT TO THE SIXTEENTH
CONGRESS OF THE COMMUNIST PARTY OF THE SOVIET
UNION (JULY 1930)

. . . The description of the fight against deviations in the Party would be incomplete if we were to omit mention of the existing deviations in the Party in the field of the nationality question. I have in view in the first place the deviation of Pan-Russian chauvinism, and secondly the deviation of local nationalism.

These deviations are not so marked or so contentious as the "left" or the right deviation. One might call them insidious deviations. But that does not mean that they do not exist. They do exist, and the important thing is that they are growing. There can be no doubt about that. This much is certain, that the general atmosphere of the intensification of the class struggle is bound to bring with it a certain intensification of national friction, which is also reflected in the Party. Consequently these deviations also must be exposed and brought into the daylight.

Wherein lies the essence of the tendency towards Pan-Russian chauvinism under the existing conditions?

The essence of the tendency towards Pan-Russian chauvinism lies in the effort to disregard the differences of language, of culture, of manner of life, in the effort to prepare the way for the liquidation of the national republics and territories, in the effort to smash the principle of national equality of rights and to discredit the policy of the Party in regard to the setting up by each nationality of its own administration, its own Press, and its own schools and other state and social organizations.

The deviationists of this type proceed from the standpoint that with the victory of Socialism the nations must fuse into one another and must convert their national languages into a uniform, common language, that the time has come for the liquidation of the national differences and the abandonment of the policy of supporting the development of the national culture of the former oppressed peoples. They appeal to the authority of Lenin, misquoting him and sometimes directly distorting and slandering him. Lenin said that under Socialism the interests of the nations flow together to a uniform whole; does it not perhaps follow, we are asked, that the time has come to make an end of the national republics and territories in the interest . . . of internationalism? Lenin declared in 1913 in the controversy with the Federalists that the slogan of national culture is a bourgeois slogan; does it not perhaps follow that the time has come to make an end of the national culture of the peoples of the Soviet Union in the interest . . . of internationalism? Lenin said that the national yoke and national barriers would be destroyed; does it not perhaps follow that the time has come to put an end to consideration for the national characteristics of the peoples of the Soviet Union and to pass over to the policy of assimilation in the interest . . . of internationalism? And so forth and so on.

There is no doubt whatever that this deviation in the question of nationality, which takes refuge, moreover, behind the mask of internationalism and the name of Lenin, is a refinement and accordingly an exceedingly dangerous form of Pan-Russian nationalism.

To begin with, Lenin never declared that national differences must disappear and national languages be fused into a uniform language within the state before the victory of Socialism on a world scale. On the contrary, Lenin made exactly the opposite declaration, that "national and state differences between peoples and countries . . . will endure even for a long time after the setting up of the dictatorship of the proletariat on a world-wide scale" (Vol. 17, page 178, Russian edition). How can it be possible to appeal to Lenin and forget this crucial passage?

It is true that one of the former Marxists, the present renegade and reformist Herr Kautsky, maintains the exact opposite of what Lenin teaches us. He maintains in opposition to Lenin that the victory of the proletarian revolution in a united Austro-German state in the middle of the last century would have led to the formation of a unified German language and to the Germanization of the Czechs, since "the mere force of the setting free of exchange, the mere force of the modern civilization which the Germans would have brought with them, would have turned the backward Czech petty bourgeois, peasants and proletarians, who had nothing to offer but their poor nationality, into Germans without any forcible nationalizing." (See the preface to the German edition of *Revolution and Counter-revolution*.)   It is conceivable that this "conception" is entirely in harmony with the social chauvinism of a Kautsky. . . . Who is right, Kautsky or Lenin?   If Kautsky is right, how can it be that such relatively backward nations as the White Russians and the Ukrainians, who stand closer to the Russians than the Czechs to the Germans, have not been Russified in the outcome of the victory of the proletarian revolution in the Soviet Union, but on the contrary have been born anew as independent nations and are developing?   How can it be explained that such nations as the Turcomans, Kirghiz, Uzbeks, Tadjiks (not to speak of the Georgians, Armenians, Azerbaijanians, and so on), in spite of their backwardness, have not been Russified in connexion with the victory of Socialism in the Soviet Union, but on the contrary have risen again and developed as independent nations?   Is it not clear that our respected deviationists, in their chase of a fictitious internationalism, have fallen victims to social chauvinism?   Is it not clear that when they contend for a unified language within a state, a unified language in the Soviet Union, they are virtually striving for the restoration of the privileges of the former dominant language, the Russian language? Where is internationalism to be found here?

Secondly, Lenin never declared that the ending of national oppression and the fusing of the interests of the nations into one uniform whole is equivalent to the annihilation of national differences.   We have destroyed the national yoke.   We have annihilated national privileges and instituted equality of national rights.   We have destroyed the state boundaries in the old sense of the word, the frontier posts and the tariff barriers between the nations of the Soviet Union. We have established the unity of the economic and political interests of the Soviet Union. But does this mean that in so doing we have done away with the national differences—language, culture, manner of living, and so on? It does not. But if the national differences, language, culture, manner of living, and so on, remain, is not the demand for the abolition of the national republics and territories in the existing historic period a reactionary demand, against the interests of the dictatorship of the proletariat? Do our deviationists realize that the abolition of the national republics and territories at the present moment would mean the robbing of millions among the masses of the peoples of the Soviet Union of the opportunity of receving instruction through their mother tongue, would rob them of the opportunity of having schools, courts of justice, administrative offices, social and other organizations and institutions conducted in their mother tongue, would rob them of the opportunity of joining in the building up of Socialism? Does it not seem clear that our deviationists, in their chase of a dummy internationalism, have been caught in the fangs of the reactionary Pan-Russian chauvinists, and forgotten, entirely forgotten the slogan of the cultural revolution in the period of the dictatorship of the proletariat, which has the same force for all peoples of the Soviet Union, for the Russians as for the non-Russians?

Thirdly, Lenin never declared that the slogan of the development of national culture under the dictatorship of the proletariat is a reactionary slogan. On the contrary, Lenin always advocated the assisting of the peoples of the Soviet Union in the development of their national culture. Under the leadership of none other than Lenin himself a resolution on the nationality question was drafted and adopted at the tenth Congress, in which it is explicitly stated that—

"The task of the Party consists in helping the working masses of the non-Russian peoples to catch up with the more advanced central Russia; in helping them (a) to develop and consolidate among themselves the soviet system in forms that correspond to the national and social conditions of these peoples; (b) to develop and consolidate organs of their own, functioning in their mother tongue, for justice, administration, economic affairs, authorities staffed by people of their own regions who know the manner of living and the psychology of the local population; (c) to develop a Press of their own, schools, a theatre of their own, their own clubs, and in general their own cultural institutions and institutions of enlightenment; (d) to organize and open up a widespread network of courses and schools, conducted in the national tongue, both for general education and for technical and professional training."

Does it not seem clear that Lenin was fully and entirely an advocate of the slogan of the development of national culture under the dictatorship of the proletariat?

Does it not seem clear that the rejection of the slogan of national culture under the dictatorship of the proletariat means the denial of the necessity of cultural progress among the non-Russian peoples of the Soviet Union, the denial of the necessity of compulsory education for these peoples, the bending of these peoples under the intellectual yoke of the reactionary nationalists?

Lenin did in fact qualify the slogan of national culture under the rule of the bourgeoisie as a reactionary slogan. But could it be anything else? What does national culture amount to under the rule of the bourgeoisie? It is an intrinsically bourgeois, formally national culture, aimed at infecting the masses with the poison of nationalism and at consolidating the rule of the bourgeoisie. And what is national culture under the dictatorship of the proletariat? An intrinsically Socialist and formally national culture, aimed at training the masses in the spirit of internationalism and at consolidating the dictatorship of the proletariat. How can the principles of these different things be confused without breaking with Marxism? Does it not seem clear that, in combating the slogan of national culture under the bourgeois regime, Lenin was denouncing the bourgeois content of national culture and not its national form? It would be stupid to suppose that Lenin regarded Socialist culture as a nationality-less culture, destitute of any national form. . . .

Those who incline to Pan-Russian chauvinism are tremendously in error when they assume the period of the building up of Socialism in the Soviet Union to be a period of the decay and liquidation of national types of culture. The truth is the exact opposite. In actual fact the period of the dictatorship of the proletariat and of the building up of Socialism in the Soviet Union is the period of the flowering of the national cultures, which while intrinsically Socialist are national in form. They do not appear to realize that with the introduction and speeding up of obligatory school instruction through the national languages the development of the national cultures must stride forwards with fresh energy. They do not realize that the backward nations can only truly and effectually be associated in the building up of Socialism on the condition of the development of their national culture. They do not realize that it is just in this that the

essence lies of the Leninist policy of assisting and supporting the development of the national cultures of the peoples
of the Soviet Union.

It may seem strange that we, the advocates of the fusion
of the national cultures into one (formally and intrinsically)
uniform culture, with a common language, in the future,
are at the same time advocates of the flowering of the
national cultures as things now are, in the period of the
dictatorship of the proletariat. But there is nothing strange
about it. The national cultures must be given the opportunity to develop and unfold, to show their own efficiency,
in order so to provide the conditions for their fusion into a
common culture with a common language. Flowering
of cultures national in form and Socialist in content under
the dictatorship of the proletariat in a country, with the
object of their fusion into a uniform, common culture
Socialist in form and content, with a common language,
when the proletariat conquers all over the world and
Socialism penetrates all life—in this lies precisely the
logical process of the Leninist reasoning in regard to
national culture.

It may be said that such a reasoning is "inconsistent."
But have we not a similar "inconsistency" in regard to
the state? We are for the dying out of the state. And at
the same time we are for the strengthening of the dictatorship of the proletariat, which is the strongest and the most
energetic power of all states that have hitherto existed.
The maximum development of the power of the state
for the purpose of the preparation of the conditions for
the dying out of the state—such is the Marxist formula.
Is that an "inconsistency"? Yes, it is an "inconsistency."
But it is a living inconsistency which fully and completely
reflects the logic of Marxism.

Or, for instance, the Leninist reasoning concerning the right of nations to self-determination to the point of secession. Lenin sometimes put the thesis of national self-determination into a simple formula: "Separation for union." Just consider it—separation for union. That sounds simply nonsensical, and yet this "inconsistent" formula reflects that living truth of Marxist logic which has enabled the Bolsheviki to storm the most impregnable fortresses in the region of the nationality question.

The same has to be said of the formula in regard to national culture of the flowering of national cultures (and languages) in the period of the dictatorship of the proletariat in a country for the purpose of preparing the conditions for their dying out and their fusion into a uniform common Socialist culture (and a uniform language) in the period of the victory of Socialism throughout the world.

Anyone who has failed to comprehend this peculiar feature and this "inconsistency" of our transitional period, who has failed to understand this logic of the historic process, is lost to Marxism.

So it is with the deviation of the inclination towards Pan-Russian chauvinism.

It is not difficult to see that this deviation is the effort of the moribund classes of the former ruling Russian nation to regain their lost privileges.

This reveals the menace of Pan-Russian chauvinism as the chief menace to the Party in the field of the nationality question.

What is the essence of the inclination to local nationalism?

The essence of the deviation in the field of local

nationalism lies in the effort to isolate oneself and shut oneself up in one's own national mussel-shell, in the effort to gloss over class differences in one's own nation, to protect oneself from Russian chauvinism by turning one's back on the broad stream of Socialist construction, in the effort not to see what it is that brings the working masses of the nationalities of the Soviet Union closer together and unites them, and only to see what can keep them apart from one another.

The deviation in the field of local nationalism reflects the discontent of the moribund classes of the former oppressed nations with the regime of the dictatorship of the proletariat, their effort to isolate themselves in their national state and there to set up their class domination.

The menace of this deviation lies in the fact that it cultivates bourgeois nationalism, weakens the unity of the working peoples of the Soviet Union, and plays into the hands of the interventionists.

That is the essence of the deviation in the field of loca nationalism.

The task of the Party lies in the determined combating of this deviation and in the guaranteeing of the conditions necessary for the international training of the working masses of the peoples of the Soviet Union.

That is the position with regard to the deviations in our Party, with the "left" deviation and the right deviation in the field of general policy, with the deviations in the field of the nationality question.

APPENDIX II

STATISTICS CONCERNING THE NATIONALITY PROBLEM IN THE SOVIET UNION

1. The nationalities of the Soviet Union according to the census of 1926.
2. The national composition of the Communist Party of the U.S.S.R. in 1927.
3. The national composition of the Communist organizations of the national republics in 1930.
4. Industrialization of the eastern populations of the U.S.S.R.

THE NATIONALITIES OF THE U.S.S.R.

ACCORDING to the census of December 17, 1926, the population of the U.S.S.R. was 146,637,530. On April 1, 1930, it was estimated at 158,400,000. The principal nationalities of the Soviet Union were as follows, according to the census of 1926:

Nationality.	Population.	Percentage.	Percentage speaking their national mother tongue.
Russians	77,791,124	53·05	99·7
Ukrainians	31,194,976	21·27	87·1
White Russians	4,738,923	3·23	71·9
Kazaks (Kazak-Kirghiz)	3,968,289	2·71	99·6
Uzbeks	3,904,622	2·66	99·1
Tartars	2,916,536	1·99	98·9
Jews	2,599,973	1·77	71·9

Georgians . .	1,821,184	1·24	96·5
Azerbaijan Turks	1,706,605	1·16	93·8
Armenians . .	1,567,568	1·07	92·4
Mordvins . .	1,340,415	0·91	94·0
Germans . .	1,238,549	0·84	94·9
Tchuvash . .	1,117,419	0·76	98·7
Tadjiks . .	978,680	0·67	98·3
Poles . . .	782,334	0·53	42·9
Kirghiz (Karakir- ghiz) . .	762,736	0·52	99·0
Turcomans .	763,940	0·52	97·3
Bashkirs . .	713,693	0·49	53·8
Wotjaks . .	504,187	0·34	98·9
Mari (Tcheremiss)	428,192	0·29	99·3
Tchetchens .	318,522	0·22	99·7
Moldavians .	278,905	0·19	92·3
Ossets . .	272,272	0·19	97·9
Karelians . .	248,120	0·17	95·5
Mischars . .	242,640	0·16	81·2
Yakuts . .	240,709	0·16	99·7
Buriats . .	237,501	0·16	98·1
Syrianes (Komi) .	226,383	0·15	96·5
Greeks . .	213,765	0·14	72·7
Avars . .	158,769	0·11	99·3
Ests . . .	154,666	0·10	88·4
Permiaks . .	149,488	0·10	93·9
Karakalpaks .	146,317	0·09	87·5
Letts . . .	141,703	0·09	78·3
Kabardines . .	139,925	0·09	99·3
Finns . .	134,701	0·09	95·8
Lesgiers . .	134,529	0·08	97·4
Kalmuks . .	129,321	0·08	99·3

All other populations count less than 120,000 souls.

THE NATIONAL COMPOSITION OF THE COMMUNIST PARTY OF THE U.S.S.R. IN 1927

Nationality.	Number of Communists.	Including women.	Number of Communists per 10,000 of population of the nationality.
Total	1,061,860	137,430	72
Russians	688,855	97,487	88
Ukrainians	122,928	12,001	39
Jews	45,342	11,431	155
White Russians	32,649	2,410	69
Armenians	18,088	1,070	116
Georgians	16,136	958	88
Tartars	14,711	1,314	51
Uzbeks	13,295	417	34
Letts	12,198	2,411	868
Kazaks	11,950	437	30
Poles	11,158	1,853	143
Azerbaijan Turks	10,841	413	64
Germans	5,226	718	42
Ossets	4,431	228	163
Ests	3,682	663	238
Mordvins	3,653	242	27
Tchuvash	3,539	257	32
Turcomans	2,918	86	38
Kirghiz	2,646	84	35
Lithuanians	2,577	302	621
Bashkirs	2,342	134	33

The other peoples counted at that time less than two thousand Communists, not including the Communist youth organizations.

On January 1, 1930, the Communist organizations of the various national republics showed the following national composition:

| Republic. | Number of Communists. | Included therein | | |
		Nationals of the Republic.	Russians.	Other nationalities.
Ukraine . .	250,681	131,029	71,176	48,476
White Russia .	36,308	20,148	4,283	11,877
Azerbaijan .	39,892	15,709	13,254	10,992
Armenia . .	12,279	10,941	393	945
Georgia . .	34,705	22,420	3,199	9,086
Uzbekistan .	42,224	21,348	16,651	4,225
Turkmenistan .	10,448	4,225	4,585	1,638
Tadjikistan .	3,073	1,252	906	915
Bashkiria .	17,412	3,073	9,185	5,154
Daghestan .	6,651	4,270	1,742	639
Tartary . .	16,241	5,732	8,413	2,096
Kazakistan .	43,881	19,022	16,697	8,162
Tchuvashia .	3,357	2,064	1,182	111
German Volga Republic .	2,372	927	967	478
Kalmukia .	1,737	1,277	401	59

The growth in the indigenous membership has been particularly large in the Communist youth organization. It grew, for instance, as follows:

	January 1, 1925.		October 1, 1929.	
	Numbers.	Per-centage.	Numbers.	Per-centage.
Turkmenistan .	1,605	34·9	8,988	56·7
Uzbekistan:				
Uzbeks . .	11,660	53·0	42,305	59·9
Tadjiks . .	836		6,710	
Kazakistan:				
Kazaks . .	12,106	34·7	51,629	55·2

The German Volga Republic, however, showed an increase among the Germans of no more than from 1373 (34·7 per cent) to 1854 (32·1 per cent).

INDUSTRIALIZATION OF THE EASTERN POPULATIONS OF THE U.S.S.R.

In the industries of the Tartar A.S.S.R. there were employed on January 1, 1930:

21,206 workpeople, of whom 6,254 were Tartars, including 1,803 women;

2,126 officials, of whom 268 were Tartars, including 13 women;

1,262 youths, of whom 362 were Tartars, including 65 girls.

In the industries of the Kazak A.S.S.R. there were employed on January 1, 1929:

10,407 workpeople, of whom 2,595 were Kazaks, including 30 women;

2,035 officials, of whom 85 were Kazaks, including 1 woman;

1,060 youths, of whom 200 where Kazaks, including 9 girls.

In the industries of the Tchuvash A.S.S.R. there were employed on January 1, 1930:

1,969 workpeople, of whom 697 were Tchuvash, including 116 women;

312 officials, of whom 92 were Tchuvash, including no women;

163 youths, of whom 60 were Tchuvash, including 10 girls.

In the Uzbek S.S.R. there were employed in industrial enterprises on January 1, 1929, 19,809 workpeople, of whom 10,447 were Uzbeks, including 1,495 women. In Turcoman S.S.R. there were employed in industrial enterprises on January 1, 1930, 5,359 workpeople, of whom 1,005 were Turcomans, including 216 women.

Industries here comprise the so-called census industries, that is industrial enterprises with machine equipment and at least 15 workpeople, or without motive power employing at least 30 workpeople.

INDEX